FIREHOUSE CHEF

FIREHOUSE

⚔ CHEF ⚔

RECIPES FROM CANADA'S FIREFIGHTERS

PATRICK MATHIEU

whitecap

EDITOR: Jordie Yow
DESIGN: Andrew Bagatella
FOOD PHOTOGRAPHY: Jonathan Bielaski
PROOFREADER: Patrick Geraghty

Printed in China.

Library and Archives Canada Cataloguing in Publication

Mathieu, Patrick, 1978-, author
    Firehouse chef / Patrick Mathieu.

ISBN 978-1-77050-306-9 (paperback)

    1. Cooking. 2. Cookbooks. I. Title.

TX715.6.M384 2016   641.5   C2016-900627-1

We acknowledge the financial support of the Government of Canada and the Province of British
Columbia through the Book Publishing Tax Credit.

*Nous reconnaissons l'appui financier du gouvernement du Canada et la province de la Columbie-Britannique
par le Book Publishing Tax Credit.*

Canada

21 20 19 18 17 16   1 2 3 4 5 6 7

*To my wife Andrea Lauren, I would not be the man,
firefighter or chef I am without your inspiration. Everything is possible
because of you. Thank you for being my rock and inspiration.*

"You are only as strong as the woman standing next to you."

*To all of my fellow firefighters, both those heroically serving today and
those who have passed on but paved the way for others. I am very proud to be
part of this united family, especially as a member of Waterloo Fire Rescue.
Thank you to my brothers, sisters and organization for their continued support,
for being my guinea pigs, recipe taste testers, toughest critiques and
for allowing me to be your "Firehouse Chef."*

TABLE OF CONTENTS

PREFACE

There is something very unique and special about being a firefighter. It comes with great responsibility but the rewards can be immense. Firefighters are part of a family of brothers and sisters that expands worldwide. We have a bond like no other created by helping people in their time of need and by giving back to our communities. Camaraderie between firefighters is one of the greatest rewards. It is built on trust and respect as our own lives are often in each other's hands. There are many traditions in the firehouse that help build this bond. Cooking together is an integral part of culture in the firefighter family and it is one carried out across Canada. During long shifts we prepare, cook and eat together, and it is in these moments that we bond, laugh, reunite and share in the victories and failures of the shift. To me this is what builds the strength of our unity. Cooking brings the firefighting family together, it makes us stronger. For my wife Andrea Lauren and I, there is nothing more important in life than family and the time spent with each other. Families who cook together stay together, whether at home or in the firehouse.

I have followed in my French Canadian family's traditions, cooking and firefighting. My Grandpapa and great uncles were firefighters and amazing cooks in Quebec City, while my Grandmama was the chief in the family kitchen, cooking and writing recipes that would become family treasures.

When you begin your career in firefighting as a fresh-faced rookie, you go through many initiations and good hearted tests to be inducted as a member of this proud family. During meal time you are given one of two options: you either cook, or you clean. For me the decision was simple; I did not want to clean up after ten hungry firefighters. So with some sage firehouse kitchen advice from the veterans, I began to cook. Following some basic rules like "Serve the most senior firefighter first," "It better taste good," and the number one cardinal rule to never be broken, "Make sure you don't run out," I began my journey as a Firehouse Chef. I take great joy and pride in feeding my firefighter family and, for me, firefighting and cooking are passions that go hand in hand. Cooking would not exist without the firehouse and the firehouse has made me a great cook.

TOP LEFT: My brother Mark and I with Grandpapa at his fire station in St. Foy, Quebec. **TOP RIGHT:** Me, the day I realized I wanted to be a firefighter. **BOTTOM LEFT:** Our children, following the Mathieu legacy. **BOTTOM RIGHT:** Grandpapa (fourth from the right) and the original members of the St. Foy Fire Department, Quebec.

LEFT: My grandmama, the Chief in our family's kitchen. RIGHT: My beautiful family: daughter Evangeline, wife Andrea Lauren and son Luc.

This cookbook is a collection of firehouse favourites created by myself along with over 50 contributions from fellow passionate firefighter chefs from across Canada. These recipes have been tried and tested in firehouses from Newfoundland to British Columbia. They are firefighter-sized portions designed to fill, nourish and leave a little leftover, just in case a little more strength is needed before the next alarm. Let this book inspire you to get your family back in the kitchen cooking together—to bond, eat and enjoy! From our firefighter family to yours.

1ST ALARM

STARTERS, HORS D'OEUVRES AND FIRING UP THE TASTE BUDS

BACON-WRAPPED CHICKEN WINGS

30 toothpicks

30 fresh chicken wings

30 slices bacon, thinly sliced

Freshly ground pepper, to taste

1 batch BBQ Bourbon Glaze (see page 179)

IN MY FIREHOUSE you will see the barbecue being used 365 days a year. Not even icy Canadian winters will keep firefighters away from the grill! Bacon and chicken wings just might be on a firefighter's list of favourite foods so I thought, why not bring them together? These slow-grilled wings require little effort and with a batch of BBQ Bourbon Glaze the results are extraordinary.

Soak toothpicks in water for 1 hour.

Working with one wing at a time, wrap it tightly with a slice of bacon, starting at the top and spiraling to the bottom. Secure it with a couple of toothpicks if necessary. Season the bacon-wrapped wings liberally with the pepper.

Prepare a grill for cooking over indirect heat. Grill the wings on the side of the grill with no heat for 30 minutes. Flip and cook for another 30 minutes until the bacon is crisp and the wings are fully cooked. (From some blessed act of the universe the bacon will be nice and crisp and the wing should be perfectly cooked at the same time!) Just before transferring the wings to a platter, brush liberally with the BBQ Bourbon Glaze. Let wings rest for 5 minutes before serving. Drizzle wings with more glaze or serve on the side for dipping.

Remove the toothpicks and serve. Enjoy!

 SERVES 4

THYME AND GARLIC
BAKED CAMEMBERT

9 oz (250 g) round camembert
in its wooden box

1 garlic clove, peeled and sliced
into matchsticks

½ tsp (2 mL) fresh thyme leaves

1 Tbsp (15 mL) maple syrup

1 small baguette, cut into
½-inch (1 cm) slices

2 Tbsp (30 mL) olive oil + extra
for brushing

Kosher salt, to taste

In the firehouse we like to keep things simple because we never know when the next alarm is coming! Is there anything more simple or delicious than baked cheese? This garlic-studded creamy camembert is a great hors d'oeuvre to ignite the taste buds for the meal to come.

Preheat the oven to 400°F (200°C). Remove the camembert from its box and set it aside. Discard any wax-paper packaging. Take a 10-inch (25 cm) square of foil and place it in the wooden box. Place the camembert inside.

Pierce the top of the camembert with the tip of a knife and push in the slices of garlic. Sprinkle the thyme leaves over the top and drizzle with the maple syrup. Loosely scrunch the foil up over the cheese. Set aside.

Place a 12-inch (30 cm) square sheet of parchment paper on a baking tray and brush with oil. Spread the slices of baguette over the sheet. Drizzle with olive oil and sprinkle with salt.

Place in the oven with the camembert and cook both for 10–12 minutes until the cheese has softened and the bread is crisp. Open up the foil and dip in the hot baguette for a luxurious snack.

SERVES 6

BLOODY MARY
SHRIMP COCKTAIL

FIREFIGHTERS AREN'T JUST family, they are also best friends and often enjoy getting together outside of work to catch the big game—the perfect occasion to turn this famous cocktail into a famous cocktail appetizer! All of the great flavours that make up a good Bloody Mary are folded together with spicy broiled shrimp to create this super starter or party dip.

Preheat the broiler on your oven.

Set aside 1 shrimp per serving for garnish. Cut the remaining shrimp into quarters and toss in a bowl with the olive oil and Cajun seasoning. Place the shrimp on a baking tray under the broiler for about 3–5 minutes until just cooked through. Remove from the oven and allow the shrimp to cool.

BLOODY MARY SAUCE In a mixing bowl, whisk together all ingredients for the Bloody Mary Sauce then season with salt and pepper to taste. Allow the sauce to chill in a refrigerator for 1 hour or longer. Once ready to serve fold in the shrimp and divide among chilled cocktail glasses. Garnish with a whole shrimp and cilantro. Enjoy!

SERVES 6

1 lb (450 g) large shrimp, peeled, deveined and tails removed

1 Tbsp (15 mL) olive oil

1 Tbsp (15 mL) Cajun seasoning

BLOODY MARY SAUCE

½ cup (125 mL) Heinz chili sauce

¼ cup (60 mL) fresh lemon juice

¼ cup (60 mL) vodka or tequila

2 tsp (10 mL) horseradish

4 green onions, sliced

2 celery stalks, minced

¼ cup (60 mL) cilantro, chopped

2 Tbsp (30 mL) hot sauce

2 tsp (10 mL) Worcestershire sauce

Kosher salt, to taste

Freshly ground pepper, to taste

Fresh chopped cilantro, for garnish

FIG, HONEY AND ALMOND CROSTINI

Baguette, cut into ¼-inch (6 mm) slices on a bias

Unsalted butter, for brushing

12 fresh figs, halved

½ cup (125 mL) liquid clover honey (approx.)

¾ cup (190 mL) extra old white cheddar, shredded

½ cup (125 mL) slivered almonds, toasted

Fresh chives, snipped for garnish

A SIMPLE YET elegant hors d'oeuvre that balances perfectly between sweet and savoury. For my Mom, who would choose dessert over dinner any day, these are her favourite.

Preheat your oven to 400°F (200°C). Lightly butter the baguette slices and place on a parchment-lined baking tray in the oven just to melt the butter and until the sides of the baguette begin to crisp, about 4 minutes. Remove from the oven and let cool. Top each baguette slice with a couple fig halves and a drizzle of honey. Cover the figs with the shredded cheddar and top with the almonds. Place the crostini back in the oven for about 5 minutes more or until the cheese becomes bubbly and golden. Remove from the oven and garnish with fresh chives before serving.

 SERVES 6

BBQ SCALLOPS ON THE HALF SHELL

BETH EDWARDS, EXECUTIVE DIRECTOR FIRE SERVICE
ASSOCIATION OF NOVA SCOTIA

BETH, HER HUSBAND and their beloved German shepherd live outside New Glasgow, Nova Scotia and are just close enough to the Atlantic Ocean that they can enjoy the quota of scallops that we are allowed each year. I asked Beth for a locally inspired creation and as an avid diver in Nova Scotia it doesn't get much better than this!

With the vast majority of Nova Scotia being served and protected by volunteer firefighters, Beth and her association are dedicated to providing leadership and representation to the citizens of Nova Scotia in all matters of fire and public safety. Volunteer firefighters are the glue that holds our small communities together across the country. They actively raise money for local charities through fish frys, picnics, pancake breakfasts, boot drives and by sponsoring local events. This proud organization of volunteer firefighters sacrifices so much of themselves, simply for the reward of helping their respective communities and neighbours in their times of need.

Start by making sure the black sac (the stomach of the scallop) is removed. If it isn't, read up on how to open a shell without ending up in the hospital and be sure to use a proper scallop-shucking knife. Cut the black sac away. The pink and white sac is the roe, very tasty.

Prepare your barbecue over medium heat and when ready, place scallops in their shells straight on the grill. Pour a little white wine over scallops, toss some minced garlic, Parmesan cheese and breadcrumbs on top and cook for 6–8 minutes, depending on size and heat from the barbecue; towards the end of cooking scallop meat should be opaque in appearance. Serve as an appetizer or alongside a salad as a great main course.

SERVES 6

12 scallops on the half shell

½ cup (125 mL) white wine

2 Tbsp (30 mL) minced garlic

¼ cup (60 mL) finely grated Parmesan cheese

¼ cup (60 mL) panko bread crumbs

GREEN CURRY CHICKEN SATAY

1⅔ cups (410 mL) cans
coconut milk

2 limes, juiced

3 Tbsp (45 mL) Thai green
curry paste

2 Tbsp (30 mL) fish sauce

4 tsp (20 mL) brown sugar

1 lb (450 g) skinless, boneless
chicken thighs

Kosher salt, for garnish

Cilantro, chopped, for garnish

1 cup (250 mL) Quick Peanut
Sauce (see page 179)

1 lime, cut into wedges,
for garnish

GETTING FIREFIGHTERS TO experience exotic flavours for the first time used to be a challenge. The old culture in firehouse cooking was very much "meat and potatoes" and sticking to the basics. But sometimes it just takes one recipe to get your foot in the door and then you can open up the minds of the most stubborn eaters. I learned this super-versatile marinade on my honeymoon in Thailand. Street vendors in Bangkok serve up these delicious meat sticks that I thought would be perfect for my firehouse. They are a also perfect party appetizer! You can substitute the chicken for any meat or seafood you wish.

In a large bowl whisk coconut milk with lime juice, curry paste, fish sauce and sugar until well combined and smooth.

Cut chicken into thin strips, about ½ inch (1 cm) wide. Place in coconut milk mixture and toss well to coat the chicken evenly. Cover and refrigerate for 4–8 hours.

Preheat barbecue or grill pan to medium-high and lightly oil. Thread chicken onto skewers, sprinkle lightly with salt and place on the grill. Cook, turning occasionally for 7–9 minutes until nicely charred and just cooked through.

Remove chicken from grill and allow to rest for about 5 minutes. Sprinkle with cilantro and serve with quick peanut sauce and lime wedges.

 SERVES 4

THE REVERSE GRILLED CHEESE
—HALLOUMI FLAMBÉ!

Flambés make a regular and exciting appearance on my charity dinner menus at the firehouse. Not only do we offer guests an opportunity to tour our station, try on our gear and climb aboard our trucks but we try to give back to them a gourmet firehouse experience they cannot experience anywhere else, all in support of our local charities. It's not just the bright blue flame that impresses in this dish, it's the briny halloumi cheese that gets set ablaze. This is one fire we don't want to put out!

Preheat a heavy-bottomed skillet over medium-high heat. Dredge the halloumi slices in all-purpose flour, shaking off any excess. Season with pepper.

Add your grapeseed oil to the skillet and add a sprinkle of flour into the pan to test if the oil is hot enough. Once it sizzles add your cheese to the skillet and cook for a couple of minutes until nice and golden brown. Carefully flip the cheese with a spatula and cook for a couple of minutes on the other side.

Turn off your heat source and carefully pour the brandy over the cheese then ignite it with a barbecue lighter, a long match or, if you are using a gas range, very carefully tilt your pan towards the flame. Enjoy the show! Once the flame dies down squeeze the lemon juice over the cheese and sprinkle with fresh parsley. Serve immediately with fresh focaccia bread or baguette.

SERVES 4–6

½ lb (225 g) slab halloumi cheese, cut into ½-inch (1 cm) thick slices

All-purpose flour, for dredging

Freshly ground pepper, to taste

1 Tbsp (15 mL) grapeseed oil

2 Tbsp (30 mL) brandy

Juice of ½ lemon + more wedges for serving

½ cup (125 mL) fresh flat-leaf parsley leaves, for garnish

Fresh focaccia bread or baguette, cut into ¼-inch (6 mm) slices

BEEF TARTAR

M Y WIFE AND I love visiting our family in Old Quebec City where tartars are super popular, and I must say I understand why! You will see numerous versions made with beef, bison or tuna on menus across la Vieux-Quebec. For my tartar, use only the freshest beef from a trusted butcher and you will be amazed. Beef tartar is traditionally served with fresh bread and a side of French fries—you can try my Granpapa's recipe on page 168.

Place the egg yolks in a large stainless-steel bowl and add the mustard and anchovies. Mix well then add the chili sauce, Worcestershire sauce, Tabasco and pepper and mix well again. Slowly whisk in the oil, then add the brandy and mix again. Fold in the shallots, capers, baby dills and parsley.

Add the chopped meat to the bowl and fold together well using a spoon. Divide the meat evenly among 6 chilled dinner plates and, using a ring mold, form it on the plates. Serve immediately with the toast quarters, French fries and Sriracha Aioli.

SERVES 6

2 egg yolks

2 Tbsp (30 mL) Dijon mustard

4 anchovy fillets, finely chopped

2 tsp (10 mL) chili sauce

1 tsp (5 mL) Worcestershire sauce

A few dashes Tabasco sauce

Freshly ground pepper, to taste

¼ cup (60 mL) chili pepper oil

2 Tbsp (30 mL) brandy

2 small shallots, finely chopped

2 tsp (10 mL) capers, rinsed

2 Tbsp (30 mL) baby garlic dill pickles, finely chopped

1 Tbsp (15 mL) flat-leaf parsley, finely chopped

1¼ lb (570 g) fresh top sirloin steak, finely chopped

Loaf of French bread, cut into thin slices, toasted and quartered

Grandpa's French Fries, for serving (see page 168)

Sriracha Aioli (see page 181)

GARLICKY SHRIMP POLENTA
WITH ROMESCO SAUCE

1 lb (450 g) shrimp
(about 16–20), peeled and
deveined, tails off

3 Tbsp (45 mL) olive oil
+ extra for brushing

2 tsp (10 mL) brown sugar

1 tsp (5 mL) smoked paprika

1 tsp (5 mL) kosher salt

3 garlic cloves, minced

Zest of 1 lemon

18 oz (510 g) tube of polenta,
cut into ¼-inch (6 mm) rounds

1 batch Romesco Sauce
(see page 180)

THIS IS A cocktail party and tapas favourite! The polenta is a delicious and unique base to the garlicky shrimp and is topped with a firehouse-favourite sauce, the Romesco.

In a large mixing bowl combine the shrimp, olive oil, sugar, paprika, salt, garlic and lemon zest. Let the shrimp marinate for about 20 minutes at room temperature.

Preheat a cast iron grill pan over high heat. When the grill pan is hot, grill the shrimp in batches until they are just cooked through and turning pink, about 2 minutes per side. Brush the polenta rounds with a little olive oil, season with salt and pepper and place in batches on the grill pan for 2 minutes per side. Top each polenta round with spoon of the Romesco Sauce and top with a grilled shrimp.

SERVES 6

MAC AND CHEESE CROQUETTES

IN THE FIREHOUSE we make our recipes in large batches because there are some pretty big eaters, and the first rule when cooking is always have enough at least for seconds! In the rare occasion that leftovers do occur, firefighters are definitely pros at using them—no food goes to waste in a firehouse. This recipe was created to transform a batch of my leftover Stovetop Mac and Cheese (see page 106) and now the leftover creation just might surpass the original!

Spread Stovetop Mac and Cheese in a 9 × 11–inch (23 × 28 cm) baking dish lined with plastic wrap. It should be evenly ½ inch (1 cm) deep. Cover again with plastic wrap and place another baking dish of the same size on top to weigh it down and refrigerate overnight.

Cut the mac and cheese into squares approximately ½ inch (1 cm) thick. Set up a breading station. In a medium bowl, season the flour with salt, pepper and cayenne. In another bowl, beat the eggs with the milk and in a third bowl add the panko. Start by dredging each mac and cheese square in the seasoned flour, tapping off any excess, dipping in the egg wash and finally tossing in the panko. Make sure the pieces are fully coated through each process. Heat ¼ inch (6 mm) cooking oil in a large skillet or cast iron pan to 360°F (180°C), and cook pieces until golden brown, about 4 minutes per side. Remove croquettes from the pan and drain on a tray lined with paper towel until any excess oil is absorbed. Season the croquettes with a pinch of cayenne, salt and pepper and sprinkle the Parmesan cheese liberally over the top.

SERVES 4–6

1 batch Stovetop Mac and Cheese (see page 106)

2 cups (500 mL) all-purpose flour

Kosher salt, to taste

Freshly ground pepper, to taste

Cayenne, to taste

4 eggs

1 Tbsp (15 mL) milk

2 cups (500 mL) panko bread crumbs

2 cups (500 mL) vegetable oil, for frying

1 cup (250 mL) finely grated Parmesan cheese

TEQUILA LIME CHICKEN FLAUTAS

2 cups (500 mL)
vegetable oil, for frying

1 Tbsp (15 mL) butter

½ red onion, diced

1 jalapeño, diced

1 garlic clove, minced

1 tsp (5 mL) ground cumin

½ tsp (2 mL) cayenne

2¼ lb (1 kg) store-bought
rotisserie chicken, skin removed
and meat finely shredded

1 cup (250 mL) Pico de Gallo
(see page 178)

¼ cup (60 mL) tequila

2 limes, juiced

¼ cup (60 mL) freshly
chopped cilantro

1 cup (250 mL) pepper
jack cheese, shredded

Sixteen 6-inch (15 cm)
flour tortillas

Kosher salt, to taste

Avocado Lime Crema
(see page 176)

2 cups (500 mL) shredded
iceberg lettuce, for serving

MEXICAN CUISINE IS a firehouse favorite as it is fresh, fast and simple to prepare, not to mention we love feeling the heat. This recipe of crispy, fried, stuffed tortillas will most definitely satisfy and is a cinch to put together, thanks to the store-bought rotisserie chicken.

Fill a large high-sided pan with enough oil to reach about an inch (2.5 cm) up the side. Heat over medium heat until a deep-frying thermometer inserted in the oil reads 375°F (190°C).

In another pan over medium heat melt the butter and sauté the onion and jalapeño until tender, about 5 minutes. Add garlic, cumin and cayenne and cook until fragrant, another couple minutes. Add chicken, Pico de Gallo, tequila and lime juice, stirring to combine. Remove from heat and stir in cilantro and cheese. Let cool slightly.

Preheat oven to 200°F (95°C).

Working with 4 tortillas at a time, spread a heaping spoonful along the middle of each tortilla. Roll tortilla tightly around the filling and secure with a toothpick. Using tongs, hold each flauta in hot oil until firm, then release to continue cooking (flautas will float). Cook until golden brown on both sides, turning once, about 2 minutes per side. Remove to a plate lined with paper towels and immediately season with salt. Keep flautas warm on a rack in the oven while assembling and cooking the remaining tortillas. Serve with Avocado Lime Crema and shredded lettuce.

 SERVES 4–6

SALMON RILLETTES

ONE THING I have learned from my family is that French food does not have to be intimidating or fussy, which is perfect for the firehouse. My wife and I love rillettes as part of a charcuterie board, especially this unique salmon version that utilizes both fresh and smoked versions.

Season the fresh salmon on both sides with salt and pepper. In a large sauté pan combine the wine, lemon, onion, garlic and bay leaf and bring to just a simmer. Allow poaching liquid to simmer gently for about 5 minutes to bring flavours together and then add the salmon. Poach for about 8 minutes or until salmon is just cooked through and flaky. Once cooked, remove from heat and let cool.

In a medium-sized bowl whip together the butter and the olive oil with a fork until very smooth. This step is super important as otherwise there'll be big chunks of butter in the finished rillettes. Slice the smoked salmon into thin strips and cut into ½-inch (1 cm) pieces. Fold into the whipped butter mixture along with the lemon juice and the chopped herbs.

Remove the skin from the salmon and flake the cooked salmon over the smoked salmon mixture. Season with smoked paprika and white pepper and gently fold the pieces of salmon into the rillette mixture. Scrape into a serving dish, cover and chill for at least 2 hours. Let come to room temperature before serving. Serve with fine cheese and baguette. Rillettes can be placed in a sealed container in the refrigerator and will keep for up to 2 weeks.

SERVES 4–6

4 wild salmon fillets (about 4 oz/110 g each)

Kosher salt, to taste

Freshly ground pepper, to taste

1 cup (250 mL) dry white wine

1 lemon, quartered

1 red onion, quartered

2 garlic cloves, crushed

1 bay leaf

½ cup (125 mL) unsalted butter

1 Tbsp (15 mL) olive oil

½ lb (225 g) smoked salmon

1½ Tbsp (23 mL) fresh lemon juice

2 Tbsp (30 mL) chopped mixed herbs (I like chives and tarragon)

½ tsp (2 mL) smoked paprika

White pepper, to taste

5 oz (140 g) good soft cheese (I prefer Boursin)

1 fresh baguette, sliced

MEXICAN GRILLED CORN

4 ears fresh corn, husked

½ cup (125 mL) mayonnaise

½ Tbsp (7.5 mL) Mexican-style chili powder

½ Tbsp (7.5 mL) smoked paprika

1 tsp (5 mL) finely grated lime zest

½ cup (125 mL) crumbled cotija, queso fresco or feta cheese

Kosher salt, to taste

Freshly ground pepper, to taste

½ cup (125 mL) fresh cilantro, chopped

1 lime, cut into wedges, for serving

In Ontario, we really look forward to fresh corn season and in the fire-house a couple dozen cobs will regularly show up during a shift. Try this Mexican street-food edition to dress up your next cob.

Prepare a gas or charcoal grill over high heat. Grill the corn, turning frequently with tongs until the kernels have softened and are charred in spots, 6–8 minutes. Remove from the grill and allow to cool slightly.

In a small bowl, combine the mayonnaise, chili powder, smoked paprika and lime zest. Put the cheese on a small plate. Brush each ear of corn with about 1 Tbsp (15 mL) mayonnaise mixture and then roll in the cheese to coat. Sprinkle with salt, pepper and cilantro and serve with lime wedges for squeezing over the corn.

SERVES 4

PANCETTA, ROSEMARY AND YUKON GOLD FLATBREAD

4 medium Yukon Gold potatoes, unpeeled and cut into ½-inch (1 cm) thick rounds

¼ cup (60 mL) olive oil, divided

Kosher salt, to taste

6 oz (170 g) thickly sliced pancetta, diced

2 large thin flatbreads from your favourite bakery (about 9 × 11 inch/23 × 28 cm)

½ cup (125 mL) roasted garlic purée

1½ cups (375 mL) grated Gruyère cheese

1 cup (250 mL) grated mozzarella cheese

¼ cup (60 mL) niçoise olives, drained and pitted

2 sprigs fresh rosemary (leaves only)

Freshly ground pepper, to taste

FIREFIGHTERS JUST MAY be pizza connoisseurs, and it is always an easy fallback during a busy shift. This flatbread will make you put the takeout menu back in the drawer. Potatoes and roasted garlic make a deliciously unique base for this flatbread that is then topped with salty pancetta and niçoise olives.

Preheat oven to 350°F (175°C).

Brush the sliced potatoes with 2 Tbsp (30 mL) oil and season with salt. Place on a parchment-lined baking tray in the oven. Cook for 20 minutes, turning once. Set aside.

Heat a heavy sauté pan over medium-high heat. Fry the pancetta until crisp, stirring occasionally for about 5 minutes. Set aside.

Brush both sides of the flatbreads generously with the remaining olive oil and place on a parchment-lined baking tray. Bake for about 5 minutes just until the flatbreads start to turn golden brown and then remove from the oven.

Brush the entire flatbreads from crust to crust with the garlic purée and sprinkle with half of both cheeses. Cover with the potato slices then sprinkle with the remaining cheeses and the pancetta. Arrange the olives and rosemary over the top then finish baking the flatbread for another 10 minutes or until the cheese is bubbling and golden. Remove the flatbread from the oven and season with pepper. Slice and serve immediately.

SERVES 4

FRIED PEI OYSTERS
WITH LEMON CAPER AIOLI

THESE FRIED OYSTERS get their aptly named title from the Malpeque gems of our East Coast. They are crispy on the outside and deliciously tender and briny in the centre. With the Lemon Caper Aioli for dipping this is perfect for a group of friends to share before dinner.

Combine flour, salt, seasoning, garlic powder and cayenne in a bowl. Toss the shucked oysters in this mixture until lightly coated. Add the milk to the beaten eggs to form an egg wash. Dip the coated oysters in the egg wash and the toss in the panko breadcrumbs. Repeat until all the oysters are coated.

Heat the vegetable oil in a large pot or deep fryer until a thermometer reads the magic deep-fry temperature of 365°F (185°C).

Slowly dip the oysters in the hot oil and allow them to cook until golden brown, 3–5 minutes. Do not overcrowd the pot or your deep fryer; fry in batches if necessary. Drain cooked oysters on paper towels and season immediately with salt and pepper. Serve with Lemon Caper Aioli.

SERVES 6

½ cup (125 mL) all-purpose flour

½ tsp (2 mL) kosher salt

½ tsp (2 mL) Old Bay seasoning

1 Tbsp (15 mL) garlic powder

Pinch of cayenne

4 lb (1.8 kg) shucked Malpeque oysters (or Fanny Bay oysters for our West Coast friends!)

2 eggs, beaten

2 Tbsp (30 mL) milk

2 cups (500 mL) panko breadcrumbs

2 cups (500 mL) vegetable oil, for frying

Kosher salt, to taste

Freshly ground pepper, to taste

Lemon Caper Aioli
(see page 181)

PROSCIUTTO-WRAPPED SCALLOPS A LA BOMBA

So SIMPLE YET so delicious—with a fiery kick! This recipe allows the main ingredients to speak for themselves. Wrapping a buttery scallop in prosciutto adds a salty touch and once you try La Bomba antipasto (a mixture of various minced hot vegetables found in the Italian or International section of the super market) you will always have a jar on standby. We do in our firehouse pantry! These little morsels make a great appetizer, but you can also serve them over a leafy green salad for a complete meal.

Preheat the oven to 350°F (175°C).

Season both sides of the scallops with salt and pepper. Fold each slice of prosciutto in half lengthwise; wrap each scallop in a slice of prosciutto and secure the prosciutto with a toothpick through the scallop. Place a dollop of La Bomba Antipasto in the centre of each scallop. Place wrapped scallops in a buttered baking dish and bake until scallop is cooked through, about 15 minutes.

SERVES 4

12 large sea scallops (about 1 lb/450 g), tough muscle removed

Kosher salt, to taste

Freshly ground pepper, to taste

12 slices prosciutto (about 4 oz/110 g)

12 tooth picks

1¼ cups (310 mL) La Bomba antipasto, or other spicy antipasto

2ND ALARM

SALADS, SOUPS AND COMFORT FOOD

GRILLED CAESAR SALAD

DANNY FORTUNE, TORONTO FIRE DEPARTMENT,
ONTARIO

CAESAR DRESSING

2–5 cloves of garlic (depending on your taste), grated

3 Tbsp (45 mL) freshly squeezed lemon juice

1 Tbsp (15 mL) white wine vinegar

5 Tbsp (75 mL) freshly grated Parmesan cheese

1 Tbsp (15 mL) anchovy paste

1 Tbsp (15 mL) Dijon mustard

⅓ cup (80 mL) canola oil

Kosher salt, to taste

Freshly ground pepper, to taste

SALAD

3 medium romaine hearts

½ cup (125 mL) grapeseed oil, for brushing

Kosher salt, to taste

Freshly ground pepper, to taste

1 baguette, halved lengthwise

6 slices thick-cut peameal bacon (about 1 lb/450 g)

2 lemons, quartered

½ cup (125 mL) Parmesan cheese, flaked with a vegetable peeler, for garnish

MY GOOD FRIEND Danny works for Canada's largest fire department. He is one of 3000-plus firefighters that guard 83 stations in 16 districts serving the residents and visitors of this world class city. He has worked on the busiest rescue truck in Canada and spent time on Toronto Island and even on one of the department's fire boats. His crew loves his homemade Caesar salad dressing and—in true firefighter style—we are throwing this salad on the fire! Every component of the classic Caesar gets thrown on the grill. A little char on the romaine, bacon and lemon gives this classic a new twist, all dressed in Danny's caesar dressing.

CAESAR DRESSING For the dressing, whisk together everything except the canola oil until well combined. Slowly drizzle in the oil and continue whisking until a creamy dressing has formed. Season the dressing with a pinch of salt and lots of pepper.

SALAD Heat your barbecue to medium-high heat.

Cut the romaine hearts in half lengthwise. Brush the cut sides with grapeseed oil then sprinkle with salt and pepper. Lightly brush the baguette, bacon and lemon quarters with oil as well.

Place the peameal bacon on the grill and cook for just a few minutes per side to get nice grill marks. Place the romaine, bread and lemons cut-side down on the grill and cook for 1–2 minutes, until charred (but do not let the romaine get overly wilted).

To plate, serve the romaine hearts whole, surrounded by bread, peameal bacon and grilled lemons. Drizzle the dressing over top of everything to your liking and sprinkle Parmesan flakes over the plate.

 SERVES 6

ENDIVE SALAD WITH HONEY-LIME VINAIGRETTE AND SEARED SCALLOPS

THE FIREHOUSE IS most definitely a carnivore club, but firefighters also realize that we need our greens and veggies to maintain our health. So to serve a salad it better have "stuff" in it, meaning it should be both filling and flavourful. This main course salad has a lot of different flavours working: tangy citrus with licorice-hinted fennel, bitter endive and salty roquefort. And let's not forget that sitting on top is a perfectly seared scallop, making this one a show stopper.

VINAIGRETTE In a bowl, whisk together all the ingredients for the vinaigrette except the oils. Continue whisking while adding the oils in a thin stream. Keep whisking until well combined, about 30 seconds.

SALAD Remove peel and outer membrane of tangerines and cut out segments. Core and thinly slice fennel lengthwise, placing in a serving bowl. Separate endive leaves and cut leaves into thirds; add to bowl. Add lettuce and tangerines. Pour dressing over top and toss to coat. Top with roquefort and walnuts and set aside.

Heat the butter and oil in a non-stick skillet over medium-high heat. Season scallops with salt and pepper and lay them clockwise in the pan so you can remember which ones to flip first.

Flip scallops when they turn golden brown on the bottom and form a nice crust, about 3 minutes. When both sides of the scallops are golden brown drizzle the lemon juice over top, making sure to hit each scallop. Top endive salad with seared scallops and enjoy!

SERVES 4–6

VINAIGRETTE

¼ cup (60 mL) fresh lime juice

2 Tbsp (30 mL) honey

1 tsp (5 mL) Dijon mustard

½ tsp (2 mL) garlic powder

¼ tsp (1 mL) cumin

½ tsp (2 mL) kosher salt

½ tsp (2 mL) ground black pepper

¼ cup (60 mL) extra virgin olive oil

¼ cup (60 mL) canola oil

SALAD

3 tangerines

1 small fennel bulb with fronds

2 Belgian endives

2 heads Boston lettuce, torn

½ lb (225 g) roquefort cheese, crumbled

¼ cup (60 mL) toasted walnut pieces

1 Tbsp (15 mL) clarified butter

1 Tbsp (15 mL) vegetable oil

12 large scallops (about 1 lb/450 g)

Kosher salt, to taste

Freshly ground pepper, to taste

Juice of 1 lemon

BARLEY SALAD WITH SMOKY CAULIFLOWER AND PROSCIUTTO

2 large heads of cauliflower (2½ lb/1.2 kg each), trimmed

2 Tbsp (30 mL) smoked paprika

Kosher salt, to taste

Freshly ground pepper, to taste

2¼ cups (560 mL) uncooked pearl barley, rinsed and drained

2 carrots, halved crosswise

1 small onion, halved

1 celery stalks, halved crosswise

2 garlic cloves, crushed

1 bay leaf

2 Tbsp (30 mL) smoked paprika

½ lb (225 g) prosciutto, sliced into ¼-inch (6 mm) thick strips

14 oz (398 mL) can black beans, rinsed

14 oz (398 mL) jar roasted red peppers, sliced into ¼-inch (6 mm) thick strips

½ cup (125 mL) extra virgin olive oil + more for drizzling

5 Tbsp (75 mL) fresh lemon juice

¼ cup (60 mL) chopped flat-leaf parsley

BARLEY IS A nutrient-dense super grain and is perfect for nourishing a hungry crew. Firefighters have been called "smoke eaters," and it's true here as the cauliflower gets a special smoky treatment to transform this salad. It makes a great side dish, or you can make a double batch to serve it as a main.

Heat your oven to 375°F (190°C). Drizzle the cauliflower with olive oil and sprinkle with smoked paprika, salt and pepper. Wrap each head in aluminum foil and bake for about 1 hour or until cauliflower is tender. Allow to cool then cut into florets.

In a large saucepan, combine the barley, carrots, onion, celery, garlic and the bay leaf. Add enough cold water to cover the barley by 1 inch (2.5 cm) and bring to a simmer over high heat. Reduce the heat to medium and cook until the barley is tender, about 20–30 minutes. Drain the barley and then spread it out on a rimmed baking tray to cool. Pick out and discard the carrots, onion, celery, garlic and the bay leaf.

In a large bowl mix the barley, cauliflower, prosciutto, black beans, roasted red peppers, olive oil, lemon juice and parsley. Season with salt and pepper and serve.

 SERVES 4–6

LET THE SUN SHINE SALAD

JEFF DERRAUGH, UNITED FIREFIGHTERS OF
WINNIPEG, MANITOBA

Before Manitoba license plates bore their current slogan, "Friendly Manitoba," they featured the tagline "Sunny Manitoba." Manitoba may be known for its cold temperatures, but Manitobans are also known for their warm hearts and sunshine, so what's a more appropriate salad than the "Let the Sun Shine Salad." It's light and sweet, and a little different. My buddy, retired Captain Lee Harrison, gets credit for this super recipe. Depending on the fruit you select, it goes with just about anything. (Intro by Jeff Derraugh.)

Warm a sauté pan over medium-low heat. Add the butter and brown sugar and lightly brown the pecans or walnuts, about 3 minutes. As the nuts cool, wash and break up the lettuce. Give it a spin dry. Refrigerate the lettuce. Combine the dressing ingredients and refrigerate until ready to serve. We have the fruit, we have the dressing: let's bring them together! Just before serving, add the lettuce and nuts and toss them. So easy and so incredibly flavourful, this one is a keeper.

SERVES 4–6

SALAD

2 Tbsp (30 mL) butter

2 Tbsp (30 mL) brown sugar

½ cup (125 mL) pecans or walnuts, chopped into bits

2 heads of butter lettuce or 1 large head of leaf lettuce

2 bananas, sliced

1 cup (250 mL) canned pineapple tidbits, reserve juice for dressing

2 cups (500 mL) red or green grapes, sliced in half

2 kiwis, sliced

2 cups (500 mL) strawberries, sliced

3 sliced nectarines or a 10-oz (284 mL) can mandarin oranges or peaches

NOTE: Any combination of your favourite fruits will work.

DRESSING

½ cup (125 mL) canola or lightly flavoured oil

¼ cup (60 mL) frozen orange juice concentrate

2 Tbsp (30 mL) soft or liquid honey

½ tsp (2 mL) kosher salt

½ tsp (2 mL) ground ginger

1 Tbsp (15 mL) of the reserved pineapple juice

GRILLED FIG, PROSCIUTTO AND BURRATA SALAD

Burrata cheese is a soft fresh Italian mozzarella that contains a beautiful little surprise of fresh cream on the inside. If you haven't tried it, or even heard of it, you need to find it! It will be available at any good cheesemonger. If you can't find it fresh buffalo mozzarella will work great as well.

Preheat a grill pan and lightly brush with oil. Grill the figs cut-side down for 1–2 minutes, or until lightly charred.

In a large bowl, combine the olive oil, balsamic vinegar, mustard, honey and rosemary. Season the dressing with salt and pepper and whisk well to combine. Add the arugula, frisee, parsley and the grilled figs and toss lightly with the dressing.

Plate the arugula and grilled fig salad. Season the burrata with salt and fresh cracked pepper and plate a couple of quarters on top of the salad. Arrange the prosciutto slices alongside.

SERVES 4–6

12 fresh figs, halved

3 Tbsp (45 mL) extra virgin olive oil + extra for brushing

2 Tbsp (30 mL) balsamic vinegar

1 tsp (5 mL) Dijon mustard

1 tsp (5 mL) honey

2 Tbsp (30 mL) fresh rosemary

Kosher salt, to taste

Freshly ground pepper, to taste

11 oz (310 g) pkg baby arugula, large stems discarded

1 cup (250 mL) frisee or escarole chopped

½ cup (125 mL) fresh parsley leaves

1 lb (450 g) thinly sliced prosciutto

Two 4-oz (110 g) balls burrata cheese, drained and quartered

PEAR, BEET AND GOAT CHEESE GREEN SALAD WITH WHITE WINE VINAIGRETTE AND GOAT CHEESE HONEY CROSTINI

NEAL YOUNG, GRAND PRAIRIE FIRE DEPARTMENT, ALBERTA

⅓ cup (80 mL) white wine vinegar

1 garlic clove, pressed

1½ Tbsp (23 mL) honey + ¼ cup (60 mL) for crostini

½ Tbsp (7.5 mL) dried oregano

1 tsp (5 mL) kosher salt + more to taste

½ tsp (2 mL) freshly ground pepper + more to taste

½ cup (125 mL) extra virgin olive oil + 2 Tbsp (30 mL) for drizzling

Two 4.5-oz (125 g) bags mixed baby greens or spinach, rinsed and dried

2 red bell peppers, seeded and diced

3-4 Roma tomatoes, diced

3-4 beets, grated raw or steamed, peeled and diced

1-3 pears (Bartlett, Anjou or Packham), thinly sliced

2 avocados, diced

1 cup (250 mL) goat cheese, crumbled for salad + ½ cup (125 mL) for crostini

1 lb (450 g) pork tenderloin or chicken breast

1 whole-wheat baguette, sliced

THE GRAND PRAIRIE fire Department proudly celebrated its 100th anniversary in 2015. Not many organizations can claim such an accomplishment, but this ever-growing city needs their fire department's services more than ever. In the province most notable for its beef, acclaimed Training Lieutenant Neal Young offers this amazing salad, so you know it has got to be good! At Grand Prairie Fire Department they like to use the salad bar style, having each member build their own giant bowl of salad to suit their taste.

Pre heat your oven to 375°F (190°C).

Blend the vinegar, garlic, honey, oregano, salt and black pepper in a blender until the garlic is finely chopped. With the blender running, slowly blend in the oil. Set aside as you prepare the salad.

Have one member of your crew or family fire up the barbecue over medium heat. Season the pork or chicken with olive oil and very liberally with salt and pepper. Grill over medium heat until cooked through, about 17 minutes total, turning as needed. Set meat aside to rest before slicing.

The rest of your crew can set out the other prepared ingredients and place them in separate bowls. If you are adopting the Grand Prairie Fire Department salad bar method, build your own salad using your favourite ingredients (Neal recommends all of them!) and toss with dressing in a large bowl before transferring to a plate.

Place the baguette slices on a parchment-lined baking sheet. Toast in the oven until crisp and golden brown, about 7 minutes. Remove from the oven and drizzle each crostini with honey and top with a pinch of goat cheese.

Top each salad with grilled meat and serve with crostini.

SERVES 6–8

BROCCOLI STALK
AND CARROT TOP SLAW

I FIRST PUBLISHED this recipe in *Canadian Firefighter* magazine to promote using root to leaf, stalk to stem and cutting back on food waste. My wife and I hate food waste and have adopted that mentality in the firehouse as well. It was an old adage that a firefighter would eat pretty much anything; we make that come true in a good way!

DRESSING To make the dressing put the balsamic and red wine vinegars, cranberries, mustard, honey, garlic, orange juice, orange zest and salt into a blender and pulse until puréed smooth. Slowly add the vegetable oil while blending, to form a good emulsion. Add the mayonnaise and pulse until blended. Taste for seasoning and add salt or freshly ground pepper if needed.

SALAD Place grated broccoli stalks, carrots, carrot tops, cabbage, onions, cranberries, orange zest and salt into a bowl. Add the dressing and toss to combine, until the dressing is evenly distributed. Make several hours ahead of time before serving to allow the flavours to come together.

SERVES 4–6

DRESSING

2 Tbsp (30 mL) balsamic vinegar

2 Tbsp (30 mL) red wine vinegar

2 Tbsp (30 mL) dried cranberries

1 tsp (5 mL) whole grain mustard

1 Tbsp (15 mL) honey

1 clove garlic, grated

1 Tbsp (15 mL) orange juice

1 tsp (5 mL) orange zest

½ tsp (2 mL) kosher salt + more to taste

6 Tbsp (90 mL) canola oil

¼ cup (60 mL) real mayonnaise

SALAD

4 cups (1 L) grated broccoli stalks

2 cups (500 mL) grated carrots (about 4–6)

4–6 carrot tops, finely chopped

2 cups (500 mL) shredded red cabbage

1 cup (250 mL) thinly sliced green onions, tops and bottoms

½ cup (125 mL) dried cranberries, coarsely chopped

1 tsp (5 mL) grated orange zest

½ tsp (2 mL) kosher salt + more to taste

THAI GREEN MANGO SALAD

MY WIFE AND I learned this taste of Thailand during our adventures through Bangkok and my firehouse crew became Thai-food guinea pigs upon our return. Use firm green mangoes to give this exotic salad the most crunch and serve topped with the Green Curry Chicken Satay (see page 8) for a complete meal.

Purée the chili peppers, garlic, lime juice, fish sauce, oil and sugar in a blender until smooth. Set aside.

In a large bowl toss the mangoes, bean sprouts, carrot, shallots, peanuts, cilantro, mint, basil, coconut, sesame seeds and dressing. Toss well to make sure everything is coated well with the dressing. Season the salad lightly with salt if necessary.

SERVES 4–6

2 red or green Thai chili peppers, with seeds, chopped

1 clove garlic, chopped

½ cup (125 mL) fresh lime juice

¼ cup (60 mL) fish sauce

2 Tbsp (30 mL) avocado oil

2 tsp (10 mL) light brown sugar

4 green firm mangoes, peeled and julienned

1 cup (250 mL) bean sprouts

1 carrot, shredded

2 medium shallots, thinly sliced

½ cup (125 mL) unsalted dry-roasted peanuts, coarsely chopped

½ cup (125 mL) fresh cilantro leaves

¼ cup (60 mL) fresh mint leaves

¼ cup (60 mL) fresh basil leaves, hand torn if leaves are large

¼ cup (60 mL) dry unsweetened coconut

2 Tbsp (30 mL) sesame seeds, toasted

Kosher salt, to taste

BRUSSELS SPROUT, APPLE AND ESCAROLE SALAD WITH BUTTERMILK DRESSING

1 lb (450 g) Brussels sprouts, trimmed

½ cup (125 mL) pumpkin seeds

½ cup (125 mL) dried cherries

1 Royal Gala apple, julienned

½ cup (125 mL) Buttermilk Dressing, divided (recipe follows)

1 cup (250 mL) escarole or other slightly bitter green, chopped

Kosher salt, to taste

Freshly ground pepper, to taste

2 Tbsp (30 mL) chopped fresh chives , for garnish

BUTTERMILK DRESSING

1 shallot, minced

2 Tbsp (30 mL) sherry vinegar

Pinch of kosher salt + more to taste

1 tsp (5 mL) freshly ground black pepper + more to taste

1 egg yolk

Juice of 1 lemon

1 cup (250 mL) grapeseed or canola oil

¼ cup (60 mL) buttermilk

4 dashes Tabasco sauce

I LOVE TAKING advantage of produce in its prime season and Brussels sprouts are one of my family's favourites. Grating them gives this salad great crunch. The combination of the bitter escarole and sweet apples topped with tangy buttermilk dressing makes this fall salad a great surprise.

Using a mandolin or box grater thinly shave the Brussels sprouts and put them in a medium mixing bowl. Add the pumpkin seeds, dried cherries and apple and dress lightly with about ¼ cup (60 mL) Buttermilk Dressing. In a separate bowl add the escarole, season to taste with salt and pepper and toss lightly with the remaining Buttermilk Dressing.

Divide the escarole among individual plates and spoon the Brussels sprouts and apple mixture over top. Garnish with fresh chives.

BUTTERMILK DRESSING In a bowl, combine the shallot with the sherry vinegar, salt and pepper. Whisk in the egg yolk and lemon juice. Drizzle in the oil, whisking until an emulsion forms. Whisk in the buttermilk. Add the Tabasco, and season with salt and pepper. Any remaining dressing can be place in a resealable jar and stored in the refrigerator for up to 2 weeks.

SERVES 4–6

GRILLED SOURDOUGH AND CHORIZO PANZANELLA SALAD

IN MY FIREHOUSE we try to use up any ingredients hanging around and we love throwing everything on the grill! I guess there is something in the smokiness that draws us in. This version of the Italian bread salad is made entirely on the grill and serves as a great summertime main highlighting tomatoes. It's the perfect recipe to use up any stale bread that might be lying around the kitchen.

Set your grill to medium-high heat.

Brush the bread on both sides with a little olive oil. Sprinkle with the smoked paprika, salt and pepper. Grill the bread until well-marked, about 1 minute per side. Transfer to a cutting board and cut into ¾-inch (2 cm) cubes.

Next place the chorizo on the grill and cook, turning occasionally until just cooked through and well charred on all sides, about 10–12 minutes total. Transfer to a cutting board, let the sausage rest for about 5 minutes and then cut into ¾-inch (2 cm) slices.

In a large bowl, whisk the remaining olive oil with the vinegar, mustard, anchovy and garlic. Add the bread, chorizo, tomatoes, cucumber, red onion and herbs and toss well. Season the salad to taste with salt and pepper and enjoy!

SERVES 4–6

Four 1-inch (2.5 cm) thick slices sourdough bread

½ cup (125 mL) extra virgin olive oil, divided

1 tsp (5 mL) smoked paprika

Kosher salt, to taste

Freshly ground pepper, to taste

1 lb (450 g) fresh chorizo sausage

3 Tbsp (45 mL) red wine vinegar

1 tsp (5 mL) Dijon mustard

1 anchovy fillet, minced

1 large clove garlic, minced

4 medium tomatoes, cut into chunks

1 medium field cucumber, peeled, seeded and cut into half-moons

½ small red onion, finely chopped

¼ cup (60 mL) chopped fresh mixed herbs, such as basil, parsley, cilantro

SEASONAL SQUASH AND PEAR SOUP WITH BLUE CHEESE

JAMIE PIERCEY, WATERLOO FIRE RESCUE, ONTARIO

4 cups (1 L) good-quality vegetable stock

⅓ lb (150 g) bacon

2 medium butternut squash, chopped into 1-inch (2.5 cm) chunks

4 Bosc pears, chopped

2 Tbsp (30 mL) extra virgin olive oil + extra to drizzle

Kosher salt, to taste

Freshly ground pepper, to taste

1 sprig of rosemary, minced

1 sweet onion, diced

2 carrots, peeled and diced

2 celery stalks, diced

1 cup (250 mL) white wine

4.4 oz (125 g) triangle Danish blue cheese, crumbled

1 egg

½ cup (125 mL) cream

THIS RECIPE IS a great way to finish a fall or winter day of outdoor activity. It is rich, warm and full of flavour, and the complexity of its flavours allows it to eat like a meal, not just a bowl of soup.

Here in Waterloo, Ontario we are nestled in a region that produces all you could ask for when it comes to eating fresh foods. Active farming communities line our city's borders, and the climate allows farmers to produce a wide variety of excellent fresh foods. This recipe is based around one particular backyard grower who has a passion for fresh food, and I am lucky enough to work with him!

Peter Klausnitzer has dedicated over 30 years to the fire service and served as our department's Deputy Chief. There weren't many day shifts during the growing season that Peter didn't bring some samples from his extensive garden. When Peter brought in some beautiful fresh butternut squash I wanted to create something that would showcase the delicate flavour of the squash but add some boldness and sophistication to it. Like everything we do in the fire service I got the team involved. I took suggestions from other crew members and what you are about to prepare is the result of the efforts of our team. We all love the result and hope that you will too. (Intro by Jamie Piercey.)

Preheat the oven to 375°F (190°C). Place the stock in a medium soup pot and warm over a medium-low heat for later. Lay the bacon strips on cookie sheet and put them in the oven until cooked crisp, about 10 minutes. Remove bacon and set on a paper towel–lined plate; set aside.

Toss the butternut squash and pears in a large bowl, drizzle with olive oil and season with salt, pepper and three-quarters of the rosemary. Spread the seasoned pear and squash on a cookie sheet and roast in the oven for 25 minutes or until soft and golden.

In a large pot heat the olive oil over medium heat. Add the onion and cook until clear, about 3–4 minutes. Add the carrots and celery to the pot along with a little salt and pepper and continue to cook for another 3–5 min until carrots and celery are soft as well. Remove the squash and pear from the oven and add it to the pot along with the white wine. Allow to simmer for about 5–6 minutes until all the alcohol has evaporated. Add the heated vegetable stock to the pot and stir well. Allow the soup to simmer for 10–15 minutes to bring all the flavours together. In the meantime, crumble 1 Tbsp (15 mL) blue cheese in each of the serving bowls along with a crumble of the well-done bacon, reserving a little of each for garnish.

Now the soup is ready to blend. Using a hand blender blend the soup to a smooth consistency. In a small bowl crack the egg and whisk in the cream. Take 2 ladles of the soup and add it to the egg and cream mixture, whisking together to temper the egg. (If you skip this step the cold egg will scramble when it hits the hot soup.) Slowly pour the mixture back into the soup and stir well—this will create a rich creaminess. Taste your soup and season with salt and pepper to taste.

Ladle soup into serving bowls over the blue cheese and bacon. Garnish with a thin slice of pear and a few crumbles of the blue cheese and a few more crumbles of bacon.

SERVES 4–6

TOM KHA SOUP

1 lemongrass stalk

6 cups (1.5 L) good-quality chicken stock

1 lb (450 g) chicken thighs, chopped into ¼-inch (6 mm) pieces

1 cup (250 mL) shiitake mushrooms, stems removed and caps torn into bite size pieces

4 kaffir limes leaves (fresh or frozen), split in half, or 1 lime zested and juiced

1–3 fresh Thai bird's eye chilies, minced

1 thumb-sized piece galangal or ginger, grated

2 garlic cloves, sliced

1⅔ cups (410 mL) can good-quality coconut milk

2 Tbsp (30 mL) fish sauce

1 cup (250 mL) whole cherry tomatoes

2 Tbsp (30 mL) lime juice

1 tsp (5 mL) brown sugar

½ cup (125 mL) fresh cilantro

1 bunch green onions, sliced

Thai chili garlic sauce, to taste (optional, I prefer Rooster brand)

ONE OF THAILAND'S finest dishes and a firehouse and family favourite, this coconut chicken soup makes a regular appearance on the menu of my firehouse charity dinners, which are auctioned off to support local charities. It has the perfect balance of sweet and sour, salty and hot and will give any menu a special exotic feel. You can substitute the chicken for shrimp, if you prefer.

Pound the lower portion of the lemongrass stalk with the back side of your knife then finely slice. Retain the upper stalk for the soup pot to stir. Place chicken stock in a large soup pot over medium-high heat and bring to a boil. Add the chicken, mushrooms, the prepared lemongrass, kaffir lime leaves and the chili. Reduce heat and simmer gently for 5–8 minutes or until chicken is just cooked. Add the galangal (or ginger), garlic, coconut milk, fish sauce and cherry tomatoes. Stir well and simmer gently for about 5 minutes. Turn the heat down to minimum and add the lime juice and sugar, stirring well. Do a taste test looking for a balance between spicy, sour, salty and sweet flavours. Add more fish sauce if not salty or flavourful enough. If too sour from the lime, add more sugar. If too spicy or if you'd like it creamier, add more coconut milk. If not spicy enough, add more chili peppers.

Ladle the soup into serving bowls and sprinkle cilantro and green onions over each bowl. For an extra kick of fiery flavour, add a dollop of Thai chili garlic sauce.

SERVES 4–6

BEER AND SMOKED CHEDDAR SOUP

IN KITCHENER-WATERLOO we sure do love our Oktoberfest celebration, and we take the food part of it pretty seriously! This smoky, hearty soup highlights the staples of sausage and beer and is always a favourite on any Oktoberfest menu. Use a full-bodied brew to really bring out the flavour.

In a large saucepan cook the sausage in a little touch of oil over moderate heat until the fat is rendered and the sausage is beginning to crisp, about 7 minutes. Using a slotted spoon, transfer the sausage to a bowl. Add the celery, onion, jalapeño, garlic and thyme to the saucepan and cook over moderate heat, stirring until softened, about 8 minutes. Add half of the beer and cook until reduced by half, about 5 minutes. Add the chicken stock and bring to a simmer.

In a separate small skillet, melt the butter. Add the flour and cook over moderate heat, stirring until lightly browned, about 2 minutes. Whisk this roux into the soup until incorporated and bring to a simmer. Cook until thickened, about 8 minutes. Add the milk and the remaining beer. Add the cheddar cheeses a handful at a time, simmering and stirring occasionally until thick and creamy, about 5 minutes. Stir in the sausage and season with salt, pepper and smoked paprika. Add more beer or stock if the soup is too thick. Garnish with fresh green onion and serve right away.

SERVES 4–6

1 lb (450 g) German smoked sausage, diced into ⅓-inch (8 mm) pieces

1 celery stalk, finely chopped

1 small onion, finely chopped

1 large jalapeño, seeded and chopped

2 large garlic cloves, minced

1 Tbsp (15 mL) chopped thyme

1 tallboy can (16 oz/470 mL) dark beer, divided

2¼ cups (560 mL) low-sodium chicken stock (approx.)

¼ cup (60 mL) unsalted butter

¼ cup (60 mL) all-purpose flour

½ cup (125 mL) milk

1 cup (250 mL) coarsely shredded sharp yellow aged cheddar cheese

½ cup (125 mL) coarsely shredded smoked cheddar cheese

Kosher salt, to taste

Freshly ground pepper, to taste

Smoked paprika, to taste

1 green onion, sliced for garnish

WILD MUSHROOM BISQUE

2 oz (60 g) dried morel
or porcini mushrooms

3 cups (750 mL) warm water

¼ cup (60 mL) unsalted butter

1 Tbsp (15 mL) extra
virgin olive oil

½ cup (125 mL) chopped shallots

½ lb (225 g) mixed fresh
mushrooms (button, cremini
and shitake), coarsely chopped

Kosher salt, to taste

Freshly ground pepper, to taste

1 Tbsp (15 mL) fresh
thyme leaves

Pinch of freshly grated nutmeg

3 Tbsp (45 mL) all-purpose
flour

4 cups (1 L) vegetable stock

½ cup (125 mL) light
cream (or more)

1 Tbsp (15 mL) snipped
fresh chives

2-3 Tbsp (30-45 mL) truffle oil,
for garnish (optional)

IN THE FIREHOUSE we love meals that get better and better the longer they cook. That's probably why we love our soups so much. A big pot can be put on the stove and allowed the time it needs for flavour to develop, and we know if we have an alarm there is a comforting bowl of soup waiting for us when we get back! It is hard to beat the rich earthy flavour of this bisque. It derives intense mushroom flavour by using a mix of fresh and dried mushrooms as well as a mushroom broth.

Soak the dried mushrooms in warm water until softened, about 20–30 minutes.

Drain the mushrooms, reserving the liquid used for soaking. Chop coarsely and discard any tough stems. Strain the soaking liquid and set aside.

Melt butter in the olive oil in a large saucepan over medium heat. Add the shallots and cook, stirring occasionally until soft, about 3 minutes. Add the dried and fresh mushrooms, salt and pepper, thyme and nutmeg. Cook until most of the mushroom liquid evaporates, about 6–8 minutes. Add the flour and stir continuously until a blonde roux is formed, about 5 minutes. Whisk in stock and about 2 cups (500 mL) mushroom soaking liquid. Bring to boil whisking often, then reduce the heat to simmer gently until soup thickens, about 20 minutes.

Whisk cream into the soup and simmer for about 5 minutes to warm. If desired, thin soup with any remaining mushroom soaking liquid and more cream. Taste the soup and season with salt and pepper if necessary. Sprinkle with chives and drizzle with truffle oil just before serving.

SERVES 4–6

TACO CHICKEN SOUP

JEFF DERRAUGH, UNITED FIREFIGHTERS
OF WINNIPEG, MANITOBA

1 batch Cuban Lime Marinade
(recipe follows)

2 lb (900 g) boneless chicken
or turkey thighs or breasts

1 Tbsp (15 mL) butter

1 medium onion, diced

2 celery stalks, diced

2 carrots, sliced thin

Kosher salt, to taste

Freshly ground pepper, to taste

1 orange or red bell
pepper, diced

4 cups (1 L) chicken stock

3 cups (750 mL) salsa (I love
smoky chipotle salsa)

19 oz (540 mL) can kidney or
black beans, rinsed

11 oz (310 g) can peaches-and-
cream corn

1 cup (250 mL) sour cream,
for garnish

A couple taco chips for each
bowl, for garnish

½ cup (125 mL) chopped fresh
cilantro, for garnish

WINTERS ARE ALL about soup lunches in Winterpeg. Try fighting a fire at 40 below and you'll see what I mean! Fire Hall #4, where I'm currently stationed, is home to the annual Rooftop Campout Boot Drive for Muscular Dystrophy. If you picture this held under sunny summer skies, well, you'd be underestimating our Manitoba macho. No, we wait until the absolute dead of winter to maximize the challenge and voluntarily pitch a tent on the hall's roof, all in support of Muscular Dystrophy. When we finally come down off the roof we look for any means to warm our bones.

This is a great firehall soup because, save the marinating time, it comes together in a flash even though it tastes like it's been simmering for hours. It's so flavourful that you likely won't even need to do the standard salt-and-pepper tune-up before serving, as the salsa takes care of all the seasoning you'll ever need. Olé! (Intro by Jeff Derraugh.)

Marinate the chicken in the Cuban Lime Marinade for at least 4 hours, but preferably overnight, to maximize flavours. If you're in a rush, then simply season with a healthy shot of Fired-Up Santa Fe Spice (see page 112) instead. Barbecue or broil the thighs over medium heat until cooked through.

Cut the chicken into bite-sized pieces. You measured everyone's mouths ahead of time, didn't you?

Toss the butter into a soup pot over medium heat and get the onion in there, frying it up until caramelized or, in blue-collar layman terms understood best by people like me, slightly browned.

Pull the celery and carrots from the on-deck circle and toss them in. Season the veggies with salt and pepper and fry until tender-crisp.

The peppers are wanting in on the veggie fest, so acquaint them with the others and fry briefly, just long enough to slightly soften and flavourize.

Pour in the chicken broth, salsa, beans and corn. Bring your soup to a simmer and get the cooked chicken in there to round out the lineup.

Heat the soup through for at least 15 minutes to combine the flavours—as usual, the longer they meld, the better the soup will be.

Ladle the soup into bowls. Place a dollop of sour cream in the centre of each bowl, stand the taco chips around the inside rim and sprinkle chopped cilantro over top. Talk about presentation! Is this a high-class Tex-Mex restaurant you're running here, or what?

CUBAN LIME MARINADE Mash the garlic with the salt and add the oregano, cumin and cayenne. Whisk in the lime juice and olive oil. Marinate away! (This marinade is good for 2 lb/900 g of meat.)

SERVES 4–6

CUBAN LIME MARINADE

10 garlic cloves, crushed

½ Tbsp (7.5 mL) kosher salt

2 Tbsp (30 mL) dried oregano

1 Tbsp (15 mL) ground cumin

½ tsp (2 mL) cayenne

1 cup (250 mL) lime juice (fresh is best, but I'll accept the bottled stuff)

⅓ cup (80 mL) extra virgin olive oil

CIOPPINO

STOCK

2 Tbsp (30 mL) olive oil

1 medium onion, finely chopped

4 garlic cloves, chopped

1 tsp (5 mL) dried basil

1 tsp (5 mL) dried oregano

½ tsp (2 mL) red chili pepper flakes

1 cup (250 mL) dry white wine

28 oz (796 mL) can whole San Marzano tomatoes with juices

2 cups (500 mL) clam juice

4 sprigs flat-leaf parsley, chopped

2 bay leaves

8 cups (2 L) good-quality vegetable stock

Kosher salt, to taste

Freshly ground pepper, to taste

SOUP

2 Tbsp (30 mL) olive oil

1 medium shallot, finely chopped

2 garlic cloves, thinly sliced

2 lb (900 g) any mix of mussels, clams or cockles, scrubbed and debearded

¼ cup (60 mL) dry white wine

1 lb (450 g) haddock, cut into 1-inch (2.5 cm) pieces

1 lb (450 g) large shrimp, peeled, deveined and tails removed

1 lb (450 g) bay scallops

¼ cup (60 mL) unsalted butter, cut into cubes

IF YOU AND your crew love seafood then this hearty fisherman's stew is perfect for you! You can use any combination of seafood you wish and, served with some garlic-y sourdough bread, you have an amazing one-pot meal. This hearty seafood stew is a favourite in our house. Once you have the stock prepared it's a cinch, just add any seafood you wish to the pot.

STOCK To make the stock, heat the oil in a large soup pot over medium heat. Add the onion and cook, stirring occasionally until softened, about 8–10 minutes. Add the garlic, basil, oregano and chili flakes and stir until fragrant, about 3 minutes. Add the wine and bring to a boil. Lower heat to maintain a simmer and cook until the wine is reduced by half, about 4 minutes. Add tomatoes with their juices and cook, stirring occasionally until the stock has thickened, 15–20 minutes. Add clam juice, parsley, bay leaves and the vegetable stock, season with salt and pepper. Simmer until all the flavours meld, about 10–15 minutes more. Now prepare the rest of the soup.

SOUP In another large soup pot heat the oil over medium heat. Add the shallot and cook until softened, about 3 minutes. Add the garlic and cook until just fragrant, about 1 minute. Add the mussels, clams or cockles, and the wine. Cover and cook over medium-high heat, stirring occasionally, until the shells have opened, about 4 minutes. Discard any shells that have not opened. Add the reserved stock and bring to a simmer. Add the fish, shrimp and scallops. Cover and cook just until opaque, about 4 minutes. Don't overcook! Stir in the butter and season with salt and pepper. Divide among bowls and top with fresh parsley. Serve with sourdough toast.

🧯 SERVES 4–6

Kosher salt, to taste

Freshly ground pepper, to taste

½ cup (125 mL) chopped flat-leaf parsley

1 loaf sourdough bread, sliced ½ inch (1 cm) thick, toasted and brushed with oil, for serving

BALSAMIC ROASTED BEET SOUP WITH WALNUTS, BLUE CHEESE AND LIME CREMA

ROASTING THE BEETS really brings out their earthy sweetness, but it's the added toppings that really make this soup pop. This is a great winter soup when beets are at their freshest.

Preheat your oven to 400°F (200°C).

Drizzle beets with olive oil and balsamic vinegar, season with salt and pepper and roast in foil lined with parchment paper until tender, about 1 hour. Meanwhile, drizzle garlic cloves with oil and roast in separate foil packet, about 30 minutes. Set aside.

Heat 2 Tbsp (30 mL) olive oil and butter in a pot over medium heat. Add leek and cook stirring until tender, about 6–8 minutes. Add roasted beets and garlic, thyme, bay leaf and vegetable stock. Season the soup to taste with salt and pepper. Bring to a boil and then reduce heat to a simmer, continuing to cook for about 5 minutes. Discard bay leaf. Remove pot from the heat then purée with a blender until smooth. Stir in lemon juice and adjust seasoning to taste. Garnish with walnuts, blue cheese, fresh chives and a drizzle of Lime Crema.

LIME CREMA In a small bowl whisk all ingredients together until well combined and smooth.

SERVES 4–6

3 medium beets

2 Tbsp (30 mL) olive oil +
2 Tbsp (30 mL) for drizzling

2 Tbsp (30 mL) balsamic vinegar

Kosher salt, to taste

Freshly ground pepper, to taste

6 unpeeled garlic cloves

1 Tbsp (15 mL) butter

1 large leek, thinly sliced

1 tsp (5 mL) fresh thyme leaves

1 bay leaf

4 cups (1 L) vegetable stock

2 Tbsp (30 mL) lemon juice

½ cup (125 mL) walnut pieces, toasted

4.4 oz (130 mL) triangle Danish blue cheese, crumbled

¼ cup (60 mL) fresh chives, chopped

1 batch Lime Crema (recipe follows)

LIME CREMA

1 cup (250 mL) crema or thick sour cream

¼ cup (60 mL) heavy cream

1 lime, juiced

Kosher salt, to taste

White pepper, to taste

1 Tbsp (15 mL) chopped chives

CLASSIC FRENCH ONION SOUP

½ cup (125 mL)
unsalted butter

1 Tbsp (15 mL) olive oil

4 onions, sliced (a mix of red
and sweet onions)

2 garlic cloves, chopped

2 bay leaves

2 fresh thyme sprigs

Kosher salt, to taste

Freshly ground pepper, to taste

1 cup (250 mL) good-quality
red wine (I like a Bordeaux)

3 heaping Tbsp (50 mL)
all-purpose flour

8 cups (2 L) beef broth

1 baguette, sliced

1 cup (250 mL) grated
Gruyère cheese

When I was a kid, if I ever saw French onion soup on a menu I had to order it. I will thank my French-Canadian roots for that, but I thought I better learn to prepare my own. It is now a firehouse classic as it is a cinch to prepare and is at its best when allowed to just simmer away. If you don't have gratin bowls, don't sweat it, this recipe allows you to enjoy the French bistro classic in any type of bowl.

Melt the butter in the oil in a large soup pot over medium heat. Add the onions, garlic, bay leaves, thyme, salt and pepper and cook until the onions are very soft and caramelized, about 25 minutes. Add the wine and bring to a boil, reduce the heat and simmer until the wine has absorbed into the onions, about 5 minutes. Discard the bay leaves and thyme sprigs. Dust the onions with the flour and give them a stir. Turn the heat down to medium-low so the flour doesn't burn, and cook for 10 minutes forming a blonde roux. Now slowly add the beef broth and bring the soup back to a simmer. Continue simmering for about 10 minutes so that all the flavours come together; season to taste with salt and pepper. The longer you simmer the soup the more depth the broth will have. If you have the time, simmer away for a couple of hours!

When you're ready to eat, preheat the broiler. Arrange the baguette slices on a baking tray in a single layer. Sprinkle the slices with the Gruyère and broil until bubbly and golden brown, 3–5 minutes. Ladle the soup in bowls and float several of the Gruyère croutons on top.

Alternatively, ladle the soup into oven-safe gratin bowls, top each with 2 slices of bread and top with cheese. Put the bowls into the oven to toast the bread and melt the cheese.

SERVES 4–6

CURRIED CAULIFLOWER AND LENTIL SOUP

WE TRY TO incorporate a healthy balance of vegetables in our diets at the firehouse. This Indian-inspired soup serves as a hearty vegetarian main. Protein from the lentils to nourish and keep us strong along with the ginger and spices will definitely help to keep the common cold away.

Rinse the lentils several times in cold water. In a large bowl, cover them with boiling water. Allow them to sit while you continue.

Heat your soup pot over medium heat and add the ghee or oil and butter. Add the onion and salt. Cook for a few minutes over medium heat stirring frequently. When the onion is soft and translucent add the ginger, garlic and the ground spices. Stir as you cook over medium heat for a couple minutes until the spices become fragrant.

Pour the lentils and soaking water into the soup pot and add the stock. Bring to a boil and then turn the heat down so that the soup simmers. Add the carrots and bay leaves and continue to cook stirring occasionally making sure the lentils don't stick to the bottom of the pot. Add more stock if the soup gets too thick.

After about 10 minutes add the cauliflower pieces and peas, turn the heat to low, cover the pot and cook for at least 20 minutes more, stirring occasionally. Stir in the lime juice, chopped cilantro and season with salt and pepper if necessary. Serve with a dollop of Avocado Lime Crema.

SERVES 4–6

1½ cups (375 mL) red lentils

2 cups (500 mL) boiling water

2 Tbsp (30 mL) ghee, or a combination of 1 Tbsp (15 mL) vegetable oil and 1 Tbsp (15 mL) butter

1 large yellow onion, chopped

Kosher salt, to taste

½-inch (1 cm) slice of ginger root, minced

3 cloves of garlic, minced

1 Tbsp (15 mL) curry powder

1 Tbsp (15 mL) garam masala

1 tsp (5 mL) ground cumin

1 tsp (5 mL) ground coriander

1 tsp (5 mL) ground turmeric

At least 4 cups (1 L) good-quality chicken stock

3 medium carrots, cut into ½-inch (1 cm) slices

2 bay leaves

1 head of cauliflower, trimmed and broken into bite-sized florets

1 cup (250 mL) frozen sweet peas

Juice of 1 lime

2 Tbsp (30 mL) coarsely chopped cilantro

Freshly ground pepper, to taste

Avocado Lime Crema, for serving (see page 176)

EAST COAST SEAFOOD CHOWDER

Two 5-oz (148 mL) cans whole baby clams

8 slices thick-cut bacon, chopped

1 onion, chopped

2 celery stalks, diced

1 cup (250 mL) grated russet potato, skins on

1 cup (250 mL) heavy cream

2 cups (500 mL) whole milk

½ cup (125 mL) dry white wine

2 bay leaves

1 tsp (5 mL) fresh thyme

1 lb (450 g) fresh haddock

1 lb (450 g) mixed seafood, preferably scallops and lobster meat (which I think is key to making the best chowder!)

Kosher salt, to taste

Freshly ground pepper, to taste

Pinch of nutmeg

¼ cup (60 mL) chopped green onion

MY FATHER-IN-LAW retired in beautiful Nova Scotia, so when Andrea and I visit the East Coast we are always on the chowder trail trying to find the best bowl. After many, many trials I would have to say there is no bad bowl of chowder, just some that are better than others. Here is my offering to make all the East Coasters proud!

Reserving the juice, drain clams and set both aside. In a Dutch oven, cook the bacon, stirring occasionally over medium heat until crisp, about 7 minutes. Drain all but 1 Tbsp (15 mL) fat from pan. Add onion, celery and 1 Tbsp (15 mL) clam juice and cook, stirring often until softened, about 5 minutes.

Stir in potato and toss well to coat, cooking for a couple of minutes. Slowly add the cream, milk, wine, remaining clam juice, bay leaves and thyme to the pot. Bring just to a simmer and cook until the potato is softened and liquid is slightly thickened, about 15 minutes.

Stir in the clams, haddock and seafood, continuing to simmer until the fish and seafood are cooked through, about 5–7 minutes. Season the chowder to taste with salt, pepper and nutmeg. Garnish with chopped green onion. Enjoy!

SERVES 4–6

YUKON ELK CHILI WITH CHOCOLATE AND CINNAMON

OLIVER HALICKMAN, WHITEHORSE FIRE DEPARTMENT, YUKON

1 Tbsp (15 mL) vegetable oil

1 lb (450 g) ground Elk or wild game (you can use beef if wild game is unavailable)

3 Tbsp (45 mL) sliced pickled jalapeños, minced

1 Tbsp (15 mL) pickling juice from jalapeños

1 small onion, diced

2 garlic cloves, minced

15 oz (425 mL) can kidney beans, rinsed and drained

28 oz (796 mL) can crushed tomatoes

2 Tbsp (30 mL) chili powder

1 tsp (5 mL) curry powder

1 tsp (5 mL) oregano

2 tsp (10 mL) ground cumin

2 tsp (10 mL) ground coriander

2 tsp (10 mL) cinnamon

½ cup (125 mL) BBQ Sauce (I like sweeter better than smoky)

3 Tbsp (45 mL) red wine vinegar

2 Tbsp (30 mL) liquid honey

2 Tbsp (30 mL) pure cocoa powder (not Nestle's Quik!)

1 cup (250 mL) grated cheddar cheese, for serving

A couple loaves of good crusty bread, for serving

SHORTER DAYS AND cooler temperatures mean the start of hunting season in the Yukon. Although not every hunt is successful, the time spent with friends and family make every hunt worthwhile. Here is a recipe for those lucky enough to put an animal in their freezer this year. This is a popular chili I've made at the firehouse and for friends. Use elk, moose, caribou, venison, beef or whatever ground meat you have available. The cinnamon and chocolate flavours compliment the bold taste of wild game. Don't worry if you don't have all the spices. (Intro by Oliver Halickman.)

In a large heavy-bottomed pot heat the oil on medium heat. Brown the meat until almost cooked through, about 7 minutes, and drain any excess fat. Add the jalapeños, jalapeño juice, onion and garlic. Cook until the onion softens, about 5 minutes. Add the beans and crushed tomatoes and let simmer for 2 minutes. Stir in all the spices and let simmer for another 2 minutes. Now add the BBQ sauce, red wine vinegar and honey and simmer for 2 minutes more. Lastly, reduce the heat to low, add the cocoa powder and simmer for 30 minutes or longer if possible. Serve with grated cheese and good crusty bread on the side.

 SERVES 4–6

GREEN GUMBO

THE SECRET TO any good gumbo is in the roux. Don't rush this process and you will taste the difference. This recipe is another great opportunity to use any hearty leafed greens you may have hanging around or sprouting up in the garden to turn this gumbo green.

Start the gumbo by making a roux. Heat the peanut oil over medium heat for 1–2 minutes and then stir in the flour. Whisk constantly so there are no lumps. Cook the roux over medium-low heat, stirring often until it is the colour of chocolate. This will take time and patience but is worth it; this is what will make your gumbo great! Stir constantly and keep your eye on it. While the roux is cooking, bring the stock to a simmer.

When the roux is dark enough mix in the onion, green pepper and celery and turn the heat to medium. Let this cook, stirring occasionally, until the vegetables soften. Add the garlic and cook another 1–2 minutes.

Add the bay leaves, Cajun Spice Blend and slowly stir in the hot stock. Keep stirring and it will all come together to form a nice smooth stock. Add the turkey leg and all the greens. Cover the pot and simmer gently for about 1 hour and 15 minutes.

Check the turkey leg and if the meat is falling off the bone, remove it from the pot. Remove the meat from the bones, discard the bones, chop the meat and return the meat to the pot. Add the chorizo sausage and cook for another 15 minutes. Check for seasoning and add more Cajun Spice or salt if desired.

CAJUN SPICE BLEND Combine all spices together and mix well. Any leftover spice can be put in a resealable container and kept for future use in your pantry.

SERVES 4–6

---

1 cup (250 mL) peanut oil

1 cup (250 mL) flour

10 cups (2.5 L) good-quality vegetable stock

2 cups (500 mL) chopped onion

1 cup (250 mL) chopped green pepper

1 cup (250 mL) chopped celery, leaves and all

4 garlic cloves, finely chopped

2 bay leaves

1 Tbsp (15 mL) Cajun Spice Blend (recipe follows)

14 cups (3.5 L) assorted greens (i.e. kale, collards, mustard greens, turnip greens, spinach, chard, dandelion greens, beet greens, carrot tops), chopped

1 lb (450 g) dry chorizo sausage, chopped

1 smoked turkey leg (about 1 lb/450 g)

Kosher salt, to taste

CAJUN SPICE BLEND

1 tsp (5 mL) freshly ground pepper

1 tsp (5 mL) cayenne

1 tsp (5 mL) celery seed

1 tsp (5 mL) dried thyme

2 tsp (10 mL) dried oregano

1 Tbsp (15 mL) garlic powder

1 Tbsp (15 mL) onion powder

2 Tbsp (30 mL) smoked paprika

MEXICAN QUINOA MASH

NEAL YOUNG, GRAND PRAIRIE FIRE
DEPARTMENT, ALBERTA

1½ cups (375 mL) uncooked quinoa

12 chorizo sausages (about 3 lb/1.4 kg)

2 Tbsp (30 mL) extra virgin olive oil

1 onion, diced

2 red bell peppers, diced

1 jalapeño, minced

1 cup (250 mL) frozen corn kernels

2 tsp (10 mL) chili powder

1 tsp (5 mL) ground cumin

Juice of 1 lime

1½ cups (375 mL) cherry tomatoes, halved

2 avocados, diced

½ cup (125 mL) fresh chopped cilantro

IT'S ALL ABOUT teamwork in the firehouse. From the emergency scene to cooking together in the kitchen, we rely on each other in just about every situation. Neal likes to involve his crew in his recipes as it not only gets the meal to the table quicker, but also builds morale and camaraderie. For this recipe have a member of your crew take care of the grilling while a few others build the delicious Mexican-inspired quinoa salad.

Cook the quinoa as per package directions. (Substitute chicken stock for water for even more flavour!)

Preheat a grill over medium-high heat. Have one member barbecue sausages until just cooked through, approximately 8–10 minutes. Take sausages off grill and let rest 5 minutes before slicing.

Heat a large sauté pan over medium heat and add the olive oil. Place the onions, peppers and jalapeño in the pan and sauté until onions are clear. Add the cooked sausage and combine well.

Add the cooked quinoa and corn to sausage and onion mix, along with the chili powder, cumin and lime juice. Mix well to combine.

Plate mixture and top with fresh cherry tomatoes, avocado and cilantro.

 SERVES 6

BRUNSWICK STEW

FIREHOUSES ARE FAMOUS for chilis and everything-but-the-kitchen-sink stews, and I find this Southern classic to be a perfect combination of both. A warm and satisfying one-pot meal! No smoked brisket? No worries, just grab some Montreal smoked meat from the deli, or some leftover pulled pork (see Yorkton Fire Department's on page 100).

Heat the oil in a large Dutch oven over medium-high heat. Add the onions and sauté until tender about 5 minutes. Add the garlic and sauté just until fragrant, about a minute longer.

Add beef stock to Dutch oven. Stir in the chicken, tomatoes, both types of corn, lima beans, chili sauce, sugar, mustards and Worcestershire sauce. Bring to a boil then reduce heat to low, cover and cook, stirring occasionally for about 2 hours.

Uncover and shred chicken into large pieces using 2 forks. Stir in the brisket and lemon juice. Cover and cook 10 minutes longer just to heat brisket through. Serve with hot sauce and some crusty bread or corn bread to mop everything up!

SERVES 4–6

2 large onions, chopped

2 garlic cloves, minced

1 Tbsp (15 mL) vegetable oil

3 cups (750 mL) beef stock

2 lb (900 g) boneless skinless chicken meat (mix of thigh and breast)

28 oz (796 mL) can fire-roasted tomatoes

14 oz (398 mL) can whole kernel corn

14 oz (398 mL) can cream corn

1½ cups (375 mL) baby lima beans

1½ cups (375) mL chili sauce

1 Tbsp (15 mL) brown sugar

1 Tbsp (15 mL) yellow mustard

1 Tbsp (15 mL) Dijon mustard

1 Tbsp (15 mL) Worcestershire sauce

½ tsp (2 mL) coarsely ground pepper

1 lb (450 g) smoked brisket, chopped

1 Tbsp (15 mL) fresh lemon juice

Hot sauce, to taste

1 loaf of good crusty bread or corn bread, for serving

CLASSIC SLOW COOKER
FIREHOUSE CHILI

BRANDON FIREFIGHTERS, MANITOBA

BRANDON FIREFIGHTERS PROTECT the citizens of the second largest city in Manitoba with a dual-service department, offering both fire protection and ambulance services. They have been an integral part of the Brandon community for over 130 years, and the fire department's headquarters proudly houses a museum dedicated to preserving the history of the fire service in Brandon. Their firehouse chili is also classic! Simple ingredients are loaded up in the slow cooker, which does all the work. This is warm and hearty, and enough chili is made to enjoy a couple leftovers (or maybe even some chili dogs!).

In a large skillet over medium heat brown the burger, stirring often until almost cooked through, about 7 minutes. Add the chopped onions and cook for 5 minutes until the onion is soft and the burger is cooked through. Add garlic and pepper to the burger and cook for about a minute just until fragrant. Mix the burger and all remaining ingredients in a slow cooker, adding the chili powder to taste. Cook for about 6 hours on low.

SERVES 6

5 lb (2.2 kg) ground hamburger

2 large onions, chopped

Chopped garlic, to taste

Freshly ground pepper, to taste

28 oz (796 mL) can diced tomatoes

28 oz (796 mL) can kidney beans, rinsed

Five 14-oz (398 mL) cans baked beans in sauce (Brandon firefighters recommend Bush Baked Beans)

Two 10-oz (284 mL) cans mushrooms

3 Tbsp (45 mL) chili powder + more to taste

SUPER GREENS AND AGED CHEDDAR SOUP

2 heads of broccoli

2 Tbsp (30 mL) extra virgin olive oil

1 cup (250 mL) diced onion

1 cup (250 mL) diced celery

Kosher salt, to taste

Freshly ground pepper, to taste

2 Tbsp (30 mL) minced garlic

2 tsp (10 mL) fresh thyme leaves

1 cup (250 mL) fresh packed spinach

1 cup (250 mL) chopped packed kale

5 cups (1.25 L) vegetable stock

1 cup (250 mL) shredded aged white cheddar

Zest of 1 lemon

IN THE FIRE service we are exposed to many things that can harm us, not only at an emergency scene, but on the inside as well. We need to take every opportunity to protect our bodies, and we need to be good to our insides with our diets. I featured this recipe in *Canadian Firefighter* magazine as a simple and delicious way to get all the healthy benefits and antioxidants of dark green leafy vegetables. This recipe takes the classic broccoli and cheddar soup to new flavour and nutritional heights with the addition of a few more greens and the bold taste of aged cheddar.

Cut the broccoli florets from the stems and roughly chop the stems into ½-inch (1 cm) pieces. Set the florets and stems aside separately.

Heat the olive oil in a soup pot over medium-high heat until hot. Add the onion, celery and broccoli stems. Lower the heat to medium and season with salt and pepper. Cook the vegetables slowly until tender, about 10 minutes. Add the garlic and thyme cook for a few minutes longer until fragrant.

Add the broccoli florets, spinach, kale and stock and bring to a boil. Reduce heat to a simmer and cook uncovered for about 10 minutes until all the vegetables are very tender. Remove your soup pot from the heat and purée the soup with a hand blender until smooth. Season the soup to taste with salt and pepper. Add the aged cheddar a handful at a time, stirring constantly to make sure it is fully melted and smooth. Add the lemon zest and adjust seasoning if necessary.

SERVES 4–6

SWEET POTATO AND BLACK BEAN CURRY

IF YOU WANT an exotic chili to add to your repertoire, this Caribbean-inspired curry will be a perfect fit! It is an excellent vegetarian main, or it works well as a side dish to any grilled fish or meat.

Heat the oil in a Dutch oven over medium-high heat. Add the diced onion and cook until softened, about 6 minutes.

Meanwhile place the roughly chopped onion, ginger, garlic, cilantro stalks, jalapeño and jerk seasoning in a food processor and pulse until finely chopped. Add this mixture to the softened onion and fry until fragrant.

Stir in the thyme, tomatoes, vinegar, sugar, stock and coconut milk and bring to a simmer. Simmer for about 10 minutes to bring the flavours together, then drop in the sweet potatoes and simmer for 10 minutes longer.

Stir in the beans and peppers and season with salt and pepper. Simmer for another 5 minutes or so until the sweet potatoes are tender.

Roughly tear the cilantro leaves and stir them into the pot just before serving. Enjoy!

SERVES 4–6

2 Tbsp (30 mL) olive oil

1 onion, diced

1 onion, roughly chopped

1½-inch (5 cm) piece fresh ginger, roughly chopped

2 garlic cloves, crushed

1 bunch fresh cilantro, leaves and stalks separated

1 jalapeño, roughly chopped (include seeds if you like it hot)

3 Tbsp (45 mL) Caribbean jerk seasoning

2 Tbsp (30 mL) fresh thyme leaves

14 oz (398 mL) can fire-roasted tomatoes with juices

¼ cup (60 mL) red wine vinegar

3 Tbsp (45 mL) dark brown sugar

2 cups (500 mL) vegetable stock

1 cup (250 mL) coconut milk

2 lb (900 g) sweet potatoes, cut into chunks

Two 14-oz (410 mL) cans black beans, rinsed and drained

15 oz (425 mL) jar roasted red peppers, cut into thick slices

Kosher salt, to taste

Freshly ground pepper, to taste

PUMPKIN AND RED LENTIL CHILI WITH PANEER

3 garlic cloves, chopped

One 2-inch (5 cm) piece of fresh ginger, chopped

1 lemongrass stalk, chopped

1 chili pepper (Thai bird's eye or small jalapeno)

1 tsp (5 mL) kosher salt + extra pinch for the paste

½ cup (125 mL) ghee, melted, divided

2 medium onions, sliced thin

1 Tbsp (15 mL) ground coriander

1 Tbsp (15 mL) ground cumin

1 Tbsp (15 mL) turmeric

1 Tbsp (15 mL) curry leaves (fresh or dried)

2 cups (500 mL) puréed pumpkin

1 cup (250 mL) red lentils

28 oz (796 mL) can chopped tomatoes

3 cups (750 mL) vegetable stock

14 oz (400 g) block fresh paneer cheese, cubed

2 cups (500 mL) baby spinach

Kosher salt, to taste

Pepper, to taste

¼ cup (60 mL) fresh cilantro

1 roti or ¼ cup (60 mL) cooked basmati rice, for serving (optional)

IF CARNIVOROUS FIREFIGHTERS love your vegetarian chili then you know the recipe is a keeper! This Indian-inspired dish is topped with paneer, a curd cheese common in Indian cuisine. Both paneer and ghee (clarified butter) are available in most supermarkets.

Place garlic, ginger, lemongrass, chili pepper and a pinch of salt in a mortar and pestle and pound to form a paste. Alternatively, you can use a small blender or just finely chop these ingredients.

Heat a ¼ cup (60 mL) ghee in a large Dutch oven to a medium heat, add onions and the fresh paste and cook for about 10 minutes or until onions have softened and are golden brown.

Add all the dried spices, curry leaves and 1 tsp (5 mL) salt to the onion mixture and stir for another couple minutes until fragrant.

Stir in pumpkin and lentils until well coated with the spice mixture. Add canned tomatoes and stock and bring to a simmer. Cover and continue to cook for about 30 minutes until the lentils are tender. Check the chili regularly to make sure it's not drying out and add extra stock or water if needed.

While the chili is cooking, cut the paneer into bite-sized cubes. Heat the remaining ghee in a large fry pan to a medium heat and fry paneer in batches until golden on each side. Place on a paper towel to drain.

Once the lentils are tender stir in the baby spinach leaves, cooked paneer and season to taste with salt and pepper. Garnish with fresh cilantro leaves and serve with roti or basmati rice if desired.

SERVES 6–8

COCONUT AND LEMONGRASS SOUP WITH SHRIMP

THIS SUPER-FLAVOURFUL Thai-inspired soup comes together in a flash! Creamy coconut milk makes a silky stock and helps to balance the heat from the chilies.

In a large soup pot heat the oil over medium heat. Stir in the ginger, lemongrass, chili and curry paste and cook for 1 minute until fragrant. Slowly pour the vegetable stock over the mixture, stirring continually. Stir in the fish sauce, brown sugar and lime zest and simmer for 5 minutes. Stir in the coconut milk, mushrooms and tomato, cooking until the mushrooms are soft, about 5 minutes. Add the shrimp and cook until no longer translucent, about 5 minutes. Stir in the lime juice and taste your soup. It should have equal balance of spicy, sweet, salty and sour. Adjust any seasoning if necessary. Garnish with cilantro and green onions.

SERVES 6–8

1 Tbsp (15 mL) coconut oil, melted

One 2-inch (5 cm) piece fresh ginger, minced

1 stalk lemongrass, white bulb minced, stalk reserved for soup pot

1–3 Thai chilies, minced

2 tsp (10 mL) red curry paste

4 cups (1 L) vegetable stock

3 Tbsp (45 mL) fish sauce

1 Tbsp (15 mL) light brown sugar

Zest and juice of 1 lime

3⅓ cups (830 mL) coconut milk

½ lb (225 g) fresh shiitake mushrooms, stemmed and sliced

1 large tomato, cored and chopped

1 lb (450 g) medium shrimp, peeled, deveined and tails removed

¼ cup (60 mL) chopped fresh cilantro, for garnish

¼ cup (60 mL) chopped green onions, for garnish

LAZY AUSSIE VINDAROO

ROB LAURETTE, KITCHENER FIRE
DEPARTMENT, ONTARIO

6 Tbsp (90 mL) extra virgin olive oil, divided

2-4 Tbsp (30-60 mL) Vindaloo Paste (recipe follows)

2 lb (900 g) kangaroo, rump or leg

6 sweet potatoes (medium), peeled and cubed

3 carrots, sliced

2 sweet onions, thinly sliced

Kosher salt, to taste

2 red chilies, sliced (keep the seeds if you like it hot!)

3 garlic cloves, minced

1 Tbsp (15 mL) grated ginger

3 Tbsp (45 mL) white wine vinegar

28 oz (796 mL) can chopped tomatoes

2 cubes beef stock

¾ cup (190 mL) boiling water

1 lb (450 g) fresh peas

2 cups (500 mL) prepared Jasmine rice, for serving

12 oz (340 g) jar mango chutney (I recommend Patak's), for serving

8 naan breads, for serving

ONE OF THE incredible opportunities afforded to firefighters is the chance to "job share" and work at fire departments across the world. Rob took full advantage of this opportunity and spent a year as a firefighter on the Gold Coast in Australia. He brought back a lifetime of memories and experiences, a love of surfing and this amazing curry recipe using kangaroo! A quality butcher should be able to order in kangaroo for you upon request.

Heat 2 Tbsp (30 mL) oil in a pan over medium-high heat and stir in the paste.

Immediately reduce heat to low and continue to stir for approximately 5 minutes, making sure to keep the paste from sticking to the bottom of the pan. Remove from heat and let cool.

Cut the meat into 1-inch (2.5 cm) cubes. Place in a mixing bowl with Vindaloo Paste. Mix until all the meat is coated. Cover with cling wrap and let it marinate overnight in the fridge.

Remove kangaroo from fridge and let it come to room temperature, about 30 minutes. In your slow cooker layer the potatoes and carrots.

Heat 2 Tbsp (30 mL) oil in a fry pan to medium-high heat. When the oil is hot, brown half the kangaroo meat for no more than 2 minutes, turning the meat to make sure it is browned evenly. Do not overcrowd the pan with the kangaroo. You want the juices to stay in the meat and be released in the slow cooker. Searing small batches will ensure even cooking. Once browned, pour the contents into the slow cooker (with all juices) on top of the carrots.

In the same pan, heat 2 Tbsp (30 mL) oil over a medium heat. When hot, add the onions and a pinch of salt. Stir the onions occasionally and fry until they turn golden, about 5 minutes.

Clear a small space in the middle of the onions and add the sliced chilies (with or without their seeds), garlic and ginger, stirring for 30 seconds.

Now add Vindaloo Paste. Stir and fry the curry paste, ginger, garlic and onions for 2 minutes until the curry paste is fragrant. Mix the white wine vinegar into the curry. Add the tomatoes to the pan, and mix well.

Mix the beef stock with the boiling water. Stir briskly to dissolve and add the stock to the pan. Mix through until the stock is completely dissolved, then reduce to medium-low heat and simmer for 5 minutes to thicken the curry sauce a little.

Take the pan off the heat and pour its contents into the slow cooker over the browned meat. Try to cover all the meat with a layer of curry sauce, as it is the sauce that will tenderize the meat. Do not mix up your slow cooker layers at this stage. Cover, turn on your slow cooker and cook for 8 hours on low.

An hour before you are ready to eat, add the peas. Gently mix the slow cooker contents so all the vegetables and meat are evenly distributed—the sauce will thicken as it is combined. Depending on how much thicker you want your curry you can continue cooking on high, with the slow cooker half covered, until your sauce has reached the desired consistency. Note that the sauce will thicken a little further still after cooking, once the slow cooker is turned off.

Serve with rice. I prefer jasmine rice, but use what you like best. Also try some mango chutney and don't forget the naan bread to soak it all up. Throw on some Ravi Shankar, or at least Nora Jones, and chill with an India Pale Ale or your favourite red wine.

Now that's good tucker, mate!

VINDALOO PASTE Put all dry ingredients in a mixing bowl and whisk in the vinegar and oil. Keep stirring until you have a consistent paste. Unused Vindaloo Paste will store in your refrigerator for 1 month.

SERVES 6–8

VINDALOO PASTE

1 Tbsp (15 mL) cayenne

2 Tbsp (30 mL) cumin

1 Tbsp (15 mL) turmeric

1 Tbsp (15 mL) freshly ground pepper

1 Tbsp (15 mL) ground mustard seed

1 Tbsp (15 mL) kosher salt

1 tsp (5 mL) ground ginger

½ tsp (2 mL) cinnamon

1 cup (250 mL) white wine vinegar

1 cup (250 mL) sesame oil (olive oil will do as a substitute)

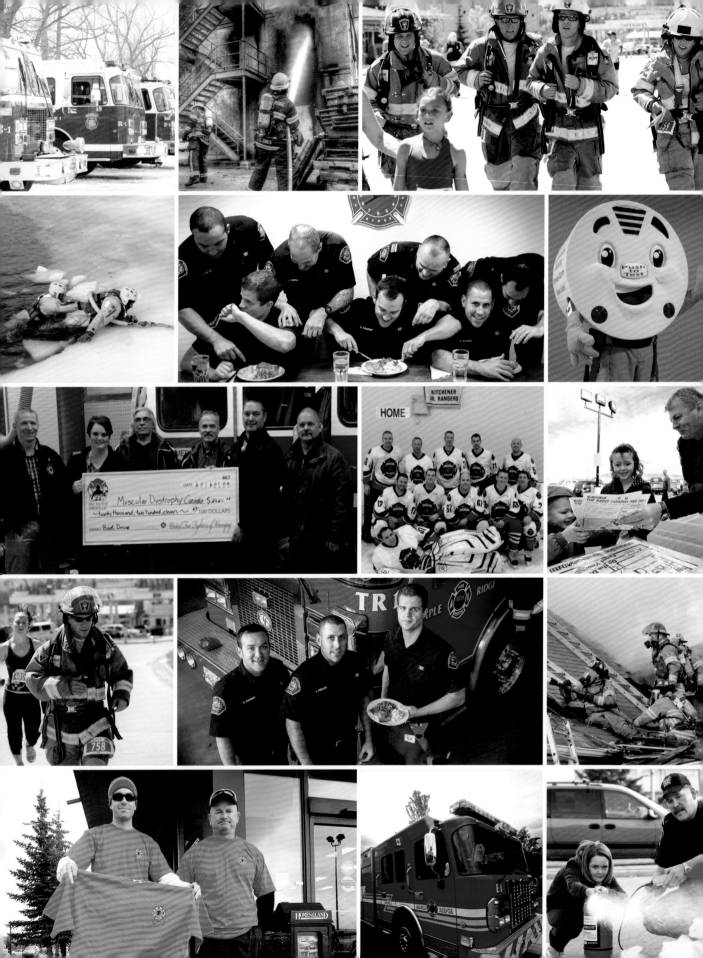

3RD ALARM

THE MAINS

TABLE OF CONTENTS CONTINUED . . .

3-MEAT 3-HEAT BURGER

1 lb (450 g) ground brisket

1 lb (450 g) spicy Italian sausage, casing removed

1 lb (450 g) pound ground pork

2 Tbsp (30 mL) steak spice

12 oz (355 mL) jar pickled jalapeños

2 lb (900 g) thinly sliced bacon

Kosher salt, to taste

Freshly ground pepper, to taste

6–8 soft crusty rolls

1 cup (250 mL) shredded pepper jack cheese

¼ head iceberg lettuce, shredded

2 avocados, sliced

1 heirloom tomato, sliced

1 batch Sriracha Aioli (see page 181)

Sometimes it's hard to remember where inspiration came from when a new recipe was created, but then after one bite it all comes back. I must say, this burger has become legendary in my firehouse. In media interviews over the years I would list it as one of my most requested dishes, as would any member of my crew when asked. I could say that the inspiration of wrapping a burger in bacon is a no brainer, but I think the story of this legend goes deeper than that.

There was a time in my firehouse when "three meats" was a catch phrase we all loved. The phrase came from our retired Platoon Chief, who would routinely book our platoon's parties based on the number of meats an establishment would serve (thanks Kennedy's Roadhouse!). Once the right establishment was found he would exclaim, "They've got three meats, boys!" We have a lot of characters in the firehouse and we do have a lot fun, especially around meal time. From the phrase, "They've got three meats boys," this burger was born.

The "3-Heat" portion of this story, which equally defines this burger, is much simpler—a batch of Sriracha Aioli was hanging around the firehouse kitchen as always, and it was very easy to add a couple more "heats" to come up with a catchy title. Now in true firehouse fashion everyone from the team has a hand in building this burger and its components, and you will still always hear as the burger is being served, "It's got three meats boys!"

Combine the brisket, sausage and pork in a large bowl. Season the meat liberally with steak spice and form into patties of your desired size—we like half pounders at the firehouse! Press a few pickled jalapeños into each patty and then tightly wrap each patty with 2 slices of bacon forming an "X." Season burger with salt and pepper and repeat with the remaining patties. Set aside.

Preheat your grill over medium heat. Sear the sliders for about 4 minutes per side, flipping just once and keeping a watchful eye as the bacon
will flare if the grill is too hot. Place burgers on top rack of your grill or
set up indirect heating to finish cooking the burgers over low heat, about
10 minutes longer. Once the bacon is completely cooked, the burger should
be finished as well. In the last few minutes of cooking, top each burger with
some pepper jack cheese to allow it to melt. To finish your burger, top with
shredded lettuce, slices of avocado, tomato and a generous spread of the
Sriracha Aioli.

 SERVES 6–8

BACON-WRAPPED FRANKFURTERS WITH JALAPEÑOS, SMOKED CHEDDAR AND SMASHED AVOCADO

2 Tbsp (30 mL) butter

2 onions, halved and sliced

Kosher salt, to taste

Freshly ground pepper, to taste

6 frankfurters or all beef jumbo hot dogs

6–12 slices of bacon

2 avocados, cubed

6 top-cut hot dog buns

1 cup (250 mL) sliced pickled jalapeños (approx.)

1 cup (250 mL) shredded applewood smoked cheddar cheese

THIS AIN'T NO ordinary dog! We used this creation to bring a stadium feel to my firehouse during the Toronto Blue Jays 2015 World Series run. The whole place was electric with excitement, as was most of Canada. It was fun to have a team of sous chefs each having a hand in making a component of this "top dog" while we cheered on our ball team. It is one of my favourite things about food, how you can use it to celebrate just about any occasion or event. European-style frankfurters take these dogs to a new level, not to mention wrapping them in bacon. Caramelized onions, smoky cheese and creamy avocado make these dogs a real treat. Game on!

Line a baking tray with aluminum foil and place a wire rack on top. Preheat oven to 400°F (200°C).

Melt butter in a skillet over low heat and add onions. Season with salt and pepper and cook, stirring the onions often until soft and browned, about 15 minutes.

Wrap the hot dogs tightly with bacon and place on a wire rack. Bake until bacon is cooked and crisp, about 15–20 minutes. For crispier bacon, broil on high for the last 2–3 minutes.

Place the avocado in a small bowl and mash with a fork. Season well with salt and pepper.

Place your dog in a top-cut bun and garnish with caramelized onions, jalapeños, shredded cheese and smashed avocado.

SERVES 6

BANH MI SANDWICHES

THIS HALF-VIETNAMESE, half-French sandwich creation has fast become one of the most popular sandwiches in the world. It has inspired entire restaurants globally, countless food trucks and now my firehouse! It is hard to explain the array of flavours that go on in your mouth, but believe me, you will understand the hype after just one bite.

PICKLED VEGETABLES In a small saucepan, bring the water, vinegar, sugar, salt and red chili pepper flakes to a boil to make a brine. Transfer the brine to a large bowl and let cool to room temperature. Add the carrots, onion and daikon and cover to keep them submerged. Refrigerate the vegetables for at least 30 minutes or up to 3 days. Drain the vegetables just before using.

CHICKEN Put the chicken in a resealable plastic bag with all but a quarter of the sweet chili sauce. Seal the bag and marinate for at least an hour.

Light a grill or preheat a grill pan over medium-high heat. Remove the chicken from the marinade and grill the chicken over moderate heat, turning once until just cooked through, about 14 minutes. Transfer to a cutting board and let rest for 5 minutes. Roughly chop the chicken thighs into bite-sized pieces and toss in a bowl with the remaining sweet chili sauce.

BANH MI Spread the cut sides of the baguettes with mayonnaise and grill for a couple of minutes to warm. Bring to a cutting board to build your banh mi. Spread a generous amount of liverwurst on the top and bottom pieces of bread. Arrange the cucumber slices on the bottom halves. Top with the chicken and then the pickled vegetables. Garnish with the cilantro sprigs and pickled jalapeño. Close the sandwiches and serve right away.

MAKES 4 SANDWICHES

PICKLED VEGETABLES

½ cup (125 mL) water

¼ cup (60 mL) rice vinegar

¼ cup (60 mL) sugar

½ tsp (2 mL) kosher salt

Pinch of crushed red chili pepper flakes

2 large carrots, grated

½ red onion, thinly sliced

½ cup (125 mL) grated daikon radish

CHICKEN

2 lb (900 g) skinless, boneless chicken thighs

2 cups (500 mL) Thai sweet chili sauce, divided

BANH MI

1 baguette, split and warmed and cut into 4 pieces

½ cup (125 mL) mayonnaise

12 oz (340 g) tube Liverwurst pate

1 cucumber, thinly sliced lengthwise

10 large cilantro sprigs

1 cups (250 mL) sliced pickled jalapeños

BLUE CHEESE-ENCRUSTED STEAK SANDWICH WITH WHISKY-GLAZED ONIONS

WHISKY-GLAZED ONIONS

2 Tbsp (30 mL) unsalted butter

1 large yellow onion, sliced

1 tsp (5 mL) kosher salt + more to taste

½ tsp (2 mL) freshly ground pepper + more to taste

½ cup (125 mL) dark brown sugar

⅓ cup (80 mL) whisky

SANDWICH

4 New York strip loin steaks (about ½ lb/225 g each)

Kosher salt, to taste

Freshly ground pepper, to taste

1 cup (250 mL) crumbled blue cheese

½ cup (125 mL) panko bread crumbs

2 Tbsp (30 mL) whipping cream

1 baguette, cut into 4 pieces, sliced in half, using just the bottoms (reserve tops)

3 Tbsp (45 mL) extra virgin olive oil, divided

1 large garlic clove, sliced in half

2 cups (500 mL) baby arugula

½ lemon, juiced

FIREFIGHTERS LOVE THEIR steak and I think blue cheese and steak go together like peanut butter and jelly. Top this ultimate steak sandwich with some Whisky-Glazed Onions, serve with a knife and fork, and you've brought a gourmet steakhouse sandwich home! This dish was one of the first creations that made me popular with my crew as a firehouse chef and is still one of my most requested meals. For any non–blue cheese lovers this recipe will turn them into believers. I still recall an evening at the firehouse when we planned to have this dish for dinner, but instead found ourselves battling a very large fire well into the night. On returning to the station and after cleaning up, our weary crew all looked at each other, then at me, and I knew the decision had been made, it was steak dinner time. Standing by the grill in the middle of the night reflecting on what transpired I felt very grateful for my crew, for everyone returning home safe and sound and for a steak dinner that was well deserved.

WHISKY-GLAZED ONIONS Heat the butter in a large heavy skillet over medium-high heat until hot. Stir in the yellow onion, salt and pepper and cook, stirring occasionally until softened and golden, 20–25 minutes. Stir in the sugar, then pull the pan off the heat and carefully add the whisky. Ignite the whisky with a gas flame or a long kitchen match and cook until the flames die down. Continue to cook until the onions are glazed, about 2 minutes. Let cool, then season with salt to taste.

SANDWICH Preheat your grill or grill pan to high heat. Season the steaks liberally with salt and pepper on both sides. Grill on each side for 3 minutes until nice grill marks form. Place the steaks on the top rack if necessary and finish cooking until the internal temperature reaches 125°F (52°C) for a medium-rare steak.

In a bowl combine the blue cheese, panko and cream. Mash with a fork until the mixture comes together.

Once steaks reach an internal temperature of 125°F (52°C) divide the blue cheese mixture between the steaks and pat it evenly over the top. Adjust the oven to broil setting. Broil the steaks for 3–5 minutes, or until the crust becomes golden brown.

Brush the baguette with 2 Tbsp (30 mL) olive oil and place on the grill for just a few minutes to get nice char marks. Remove from the grill and rub with the garlic. In a large bowl toss the arugula with lemon juice and remaining olive oil and season to taste with salt and pepper. To build your sandwich place a blue cheese–encrusted strip loin on top of a baguette bottom. Top with some whisky-glazed onions and a handful of the dressed arugula.

SERVES 4

THE CHICKEN AND WAFFLE SLIDER

SAVOURY WAFFLES

2 cups (500 mL) all-purpose
flour

¼ cup (60 mL) light-brown
sugar

1 tsp (5 mL) baking soda

½ Tbsp (7.5 mL) baking powder

½ tsp (2 mL) kosher salt

2 tsp (10 mL) freshly cracked
black pepper

3 large eggs, room temperature

⅓ cup (80 mL) unsalted butter,
melted and cooled

2 cups (500 mL) buttermilk,
room temperature

6 slices maple bacon, cooked
and crumbled

1 cup (250 mL) shredded
cheddar cheese

5 green onions, thinly sliced

Cooking spray, for waffle iron

CHICKEN

1 lb (450 g) chicken thighs

1½ cups (375 mL) buttermilk

1 Tbsp (15 mL) hot sauce
(optional)

1½ cups (375 mL) all-purpose
flour

WE JUST LOVE sandwiches in the firehouse (that's the reason why we have an entire section of this book dedicated to them)! I am always trying to keep things interesting. This is a savoury waffle, sandwiching crispy fried chicken with hints of maple everywhere. A Canadian touch on an American diner classic!

SAVOURY WAFFLES Preheat waffle iron.

In a large bowl, stir together the flour, brown sugar, baking soda, baking powder, salt and pepper. Make a well in the centre of the bowl and set aside.

Crack the eggs into a small bowl and whisk together. Pour into the centre of the dry ingredients. Add the butter and buttermilk. Using a wooden spoon, stir the waffle batter until just combined. Slightly lumpy batter is just fine. If the batter appears to be too thick add a splash of buttermilk and stir until pouring consistency is reached. Fold in the bacon, cheese and green onions.

Lightly grease the waffle iron with cooking spray and pour about ½ cup (125 mL) batter into each waffle cavity, more or less depending on size of your waffle iron. Cook until the waffles are golden brown and crispy, about 4–6 minutes. Place the cooked waffles on a cooling rack set over a baking tray. Place in a 200°F (95°C) oven to keep the waffles warm until ready to eat.

CHICKEN Place the chicken in a large bowl. Cover with buttermilk and add the hot sauce, if using. Toss together until evenly mixed and all the chicken is submerged in the buttermilk. Cover with plastic wrap and place in the fridge for at least 30 minutes. If you don't have the time, this step is not crucial but it will help make the chicken tender and juicy.

In a shallow dish, combine the flour, salt, cayenne, garlic powder and pepper. To coat the chicken, grab a piece from the buttermilk bowl, slightly drain off and throw into the flour. Pat the flour into the chicken on both sides. Return to the buttermilk bowl (with the rest of the chicken) and coat both sides. Place the chicken back into the flour, once more, and coat both sides; we're double dipping the chicken. Lay the coated chicken on a rack placed over a baking tray. Repeat in this manner until all the chicken is coated. Allow the coated chicken to rest for at least 10 minutes, this will allow the fry to dry a bit and stick to the chicken.

In the meantime heat about 2 inches (5 cm) of oil in a heavy duty pan, such as a cast iron skillet. Once the oil is hot, fry the chicken in batches. Cook for about 5 minutes on the first side, turn over once golden brown and crispy, continue to cook for another 4 minutes on the other side. Drain the chicken and place on a separate rack set over a baking tray. You can keep the cooked chicken warm in a 200°F (95°C) oven until all the chicken is fried and you're ready to serve. Make into fried chicken and waffle sandwiches with Savoury Waffles and layer with bacon, lettuce, sliced tomato, avocado and Maple Mustard.

MAPLE MUSTARD Whisk all the ingredients together in a small bowl until smooth. Maple Mustard will keep in refrigerator for up to 1 week.

SERVES 6

1 tsp (5 mL) kosher salt

1 tsp (5 mL) cayenne

1 tsp (5 mL) garlic powder

1 tsp (5 mL) black pepper

Canola oil, for frying

TO SERVE

1 lb (450 g) maple bacon, cooked

¼ head iceberg lettuce, shredded

1 large tomato, sliced

1 avocado, sliced

1 batch of Maple Mustard (recipe follows)

MAPLE MUSTARD

¼ cup (60 mL) maple syrup

3 Tbsp (45 mL) yellow mustard

3 Tbsp (45 mL) spicy brown mustard or Dijon mustard

ITALIAN MEATBALL BREAKFAST BURGER

1 lb (450 g) ground pork

1 lb (450 g) hot Italian sausage, removed from casing

1 Tbsp (15 mL) dried oregano

1 Tbsp (15 mL) dried basil

1 Tbsp (15 mL) dried thyme

1 tsp (5 mL) cayenne

2 Tbsp (30 mL) steak spice, for seasoning

1 cup (250 mL) Simple Tomato Sauce (see page 180), warmed + extra for serving

1 cup (250 mL) shredded smoked mozzarella cheese + extra for serving

4 whole-grain English muffins

1 Tbsp (15 mL) extra virgin olive oil + extra for the pan

4 eggs

Freshly ground pepper, to taste

Kosher salt, to taste

If you like breakfast for dinner, or you're like us firefighters and need a little more oomph in the morning, then this "breakfast" burger is for you!

Preheat oven to 350°F (175°C).

In a large bowl combine ground pork and Italian sausage meat. Add dried oregano, basil and thyme. Add cayenne and mix meat well without overworking the mixture. Form into 8 small patties, roughly the size of English muffins. Sprinkle patties on both sides with steak spice and set aside.

Coat a large cast iron pan with olive oil and heat over medium-high heat until just smoking. Add breakfast patties in batches and brown very well on both sides, flipping just once, about 5 minutes per side. Move cooked patties to a baking tray and reserve the cooking fat. When all patties have been cooked top them with 1 Tbsp (15 mL) Simple Tomato Sauce and a pinch of the mozzarella cheese. Place the pan in the oven while you cook the eggs, allowing the cheese to become hot and bubbly and the patties to finish cooking through.

Toast the English muffins and keep warm in the oven with the breakfast patties.

In the same large skillet heat 1 Tbsp (15 mL) olive oil and 1 Tbsp (15 mL) reserved cooking fat. Cook the eggs "over easy," allowing the yolk to still have some run in it. Sprinkle both sides with freshly ground pepper and kosher salt.

To serve place an English muffin open face on a plate and top with a spoonful of tomato sauce and a pinch of cheese. Place a meatball breakfast patty on each section and top the patties with an egg. Sprinkle with more cheese and season with salt and pepper.

 SERVES 4

JALAPEÑO KETTLE CHIP FISH TACOS

ALONG WITH THE 3-Meat 3-Heat Burger (see page 68) this may be the most requested meal in my firehouse. Once you bread something in kettle chips you may just never go back! I like to take advantage of my fellow firefighters' fishing skills; you can use perch, pickerel or any mild flavoured white fish. The go-to is crispy haddock and in true firehouse fashion it is all hands on board to help prepare the fixin's. This is also the recipe where my Sriracha Aioli was born. Wrap it all up in a soft corn tortilla and it's an awakening for your taste buds!

In a large skillet heat about ¼ inch (6 mm) of oil to 350°F (175°C).

Preheat oven to 300°F (150°C).

To set up a breading station: in a bowl season the flour with Old Bay, chili powder and pepper. Secondly, in another bowl season the beaten eggs with a pinch of salt and pepper. Put crushed chips in a third bowl. Now you are ready to bread your fish!

Dust each fish piece lightly with flour. Dip fish into eggs then toss in the crushed chips, pushing down on them to make them stick. Fry fish in oil for about 4 minutes per side or until crispy and golden brown and cooked through; cook in batches if neccesary. Drain on paper towel and season with salt and pepper

Before serving, in a dry large non-stick skillet over medium-high heat, quickly fry the tortillas for a minute or so on each side until warmed through.

In a large bowl toss the cabbage with 2 Tbsp (30 mL) Sriracha Aioli.

To serve, spread Avocado Lime Crema on a tortilla and place fried fish on top. Add the cabbage and garnish with Pico de Gallo, more Sriracha Aioli and fresh cilantro.

SERVES 4

FISH

½ cup (125 mL) canola or peanut oil for frying

1 cup (250 mL) flour

1 Tbsp (15 mL) Old Bay seasoning

1 Tbsp (15 mL) chili powder

Freshly ground pepper, to taste

2 eggs, beaten

Kosher salt, to taste

1 medium bag jalapeño kettle chips, crushed in their bag to fine crumbs

1 lb (450 g) fresh haddock fillets

SERVING

12 corn tortillas

1 batch Avocado Lime Crema (see page 176)

½ head red cabbage, finely shredded

1 batch Pico de Gallo (see page 178)

1 batch Sriracha Aioli (see page 181)

½ cup (125 mL) fresh cilantro, leaves only

MILE HIGH DENVER SANDWICH

½ cup (125 mL) unsalted butter, divided

1 Tbsp (15 mL) olive oil

1 green pepper, diced

1 sweet onion, diced

½ lb (225 g) ham steak, cubed

12 eggs

¼ cup (60 mL) cream

Kosher salt, to taste

Freshly ground pepper, to taste

Pinch of cayenne

Eight ½-inch (1 cm) slices of good ciabatta bread

1 cup (250 mL) shredded pepper jack cheese

1 batch Beer-Battered Onion Rings (see page 167)

O MELETTES ALWAYS MAKE for great sandwiches, and we always keep an abundance of eggs in the refrigerator at the firehouse so that an easy, quick meal will never be far away. I like to serve this beautiful omelette sandwich with my Beer-Battered Onion Rings (an amazing recipe and story in itself!) for a classic all-day-breakfast diner meal.

Add 1 Tbsp (15 mL) butter and a drizzle of olive oil to a large non-stick skillet over medium heat. Add in the bell pepper, onion and ham. Cook just until the ham is warmed through and the pepper just begins to soften, about 4 minutes. Remove this mixture into a small bowl.

Crack the eggs into a bowl, add the cream and whisk until all of the yolks are evenly mixed. Season the eggs with salt, pepper and cayenne. Return the non-stick skillet back to medium-high heat. Add in the eggs and vigorously mix with a rubber spatula for about 5 seconds. Continue to cook for about another minute or so to let the omelette begin to set. Use the spatula, and begin working the edges, lifting the skillet to move any of the excess egg mixture into the open parts of the skillet. Spread the remaining butter on one side of the bread slices, then place 4 pieces into a separate large skillet on medium-low heat, butter side down. Top each piece of bread with the pepper jack cheese, keeping an eye on the bread as you want it to be a nice crisp, golden brown, as well as to have the cheese begin to melt. Top each with a bit of the ham, pepper and onion mixture. Remove to a baking tray and toast the other 4 pieces of bread butter side down for a few minutes until golden brown.

Continue cooking the egg until you no longer see any liquid on top, then add in the remaining ham, pepper and onion mixture. Gently fold over, dividing into smaller sections, if necessary.

To serve, place each piece of bread with the cheese and ham mixture onto a plate and slide the Denver omelettes on top. Top with the other pieces of toast. Serve with the Beer-Battered Onion Rings.

 SERVES 4

MUFFALETTA SLIDERS

THIS NEW ORLEANS classic sandwich is packed with salty and spicy cured meats, smoked cheese and a zingy olive salad as a base. This is one sandwich that actually tastes better the next day! You can also use these ingredients to make an amazing flatbread or pizza; layer the olive salad, meat and then cheese on your favourite flatbread or pizza crust, then bake until crisp and the cheese has melted.

OLIVE SALAD Combine olives, shallots, celery, red peppers, capers, pepperoncini and olive oil in a small bowl. Stir to combine and season to taste with vinegar, salt and pepper.

SLIDERS Tear out some of the doughy insides of the bread if it's thick and lay bread slices face up on a cutting board. Spoon olive mixture on both top and bottom halves. Layer meats and cheeses onto the bottoms and then cover with top halves of bread. Wrap focaccia tightly in plastic wrap and allow bread to soak up juices for 1 hour before serving. Cut into 6 sliders and enjoy!

SERVES 6

OLIVE SALAD

1 cup (250 mL) pitted olives, roughly chopped (preferably a mix)

1 Tbsp (15 mL) minced shallots

1 Tbsp (15 mL) minced celery

½ cup (125 mL) roasted red bell pepper strips

2 Tbsp (30 mL) capers, roughly chopped

3 pepperoncini peppers or hot peppers, chopped

3 Tbsp (45 mL) extra virgin olive oil

1 Tbsp (15 mL) red wine vinegar + more to taste

Kosher salt, to taste

Freshly ground pepper, to taste

SLIDERS

1 medium loaf of focaccia, halved lengthwise

4 oz (110 g) thinly sliced genoa salami

4 oz (110 g) thinly sliced hot capicola

4 oz (110 g) thinly sliced hot mortadella

4 oz (110 g) thinly sliced provolone cheese

4 oz (110 g) thinly sliced smoked mozzarella cheese

SHRIMP PO' BOYS WITH SPICY THOUSAND ISLAND SAUCE

SPICY THOUSAND ISLAND SAUCE

1 cup (250 mL) mayonnaise

5 Tbsp (75 mL) finely chopped dill pickles

3 green onions, finely chopped

3 Tbsp (45 mL) ketchup

2 Tbsp (30 mL) whole-grain Dijon mustard

1 tsp (5 mL) horseradish

1 tsp (5 mL) Worcestershire sauce

1 tsp (5 mL) Tabasco sauce

½ tsp (2 mL) kosher salt

½ tsp (2 mL) freshly ground pepper

PO' BOYS

½ cup (125 mL) peanut or vegetable oil, for frying

1¼ cups (310 mL) flour

1 cup (250 mL) yellow cornmeal

1 Tbsp (15 mL) granulated garlic powder

1 Tbsp (15 mL) granulated onion powder

1 tsp (5 mL) kosher salt + more to taste

1 tsp (5 mL) freshly ground pepper

1 tsp (5 mL) cayenne

2 eggs

¼ cup (60 mL) milk

1½ lb (700 g) large shrimp (16/20 count), peeled and deveined

4 crusty hoagie rolls

2 Tbsp (30 mL) unsalted butter, softened

2 ripe tomatoes, sliced

Tabasco sauce, to taste

3 cups (750 mL) finely shredded iceberg lettuce

A LOT OF times a recipe starts in my firehouse because we created a really great sauce and needed to find something for it to go on top of. Crispy fried shrimp are the stars of this awesome sammy, but the homemade Thousand Island sauce takes no back seat! You can also fry up some fresh shucked oysters if available to really make this po' boy something special.

SPICY THOUSAND ISLAND SAUCE Mix all ingredients together in a bowl. Cover and refrigerate for at least 2 hours.

PO' BOYS Heat at least ¼ inch (6 mm) oil in a large skillet or preheat deep fryer to approximately 360°F (180°C). In a bowl whisk flour, cornmeal, garlic powder, onion powder, salt, pepper and cayenne. In another small bowl, whisk together the eggs and milk. Working with a few at a time, dredge the shrimp in the seasoned flour, then dip into the egg wash, then back into the seasoned flour, coating the shrimp completely. Fry the shrimp in batches until golden and crispy, about 2–4 minutes. Remove from oil and drain on paper towels.

Slice the rolls in half and butter both cut sides. Quickly broil the rolls to warm and melt the butter. Spread out the sliced tomatoes and season them with salt and a few dashes of Tabasco on each. Remove the buns from the oven and slather both cut sides with spicy Thousand Island Sauce. Divide the shrimp evenly between the 4 sandwiches and top with the tomato slices and shredded lettuce. Press the sandwich together a bit and serve your Shrimp Po' Boys with Tabasco at the table.

SERVES 4

SURF AND TURF BURGER

I HAVE ALWAYS thought that the meals I create at the firehouse are much more than just good food to fill up on—they also serve to strengthen my crew's bond, build camaraderie and maybe give us a little feeling of family and home. Often, due to our shifts or emergencies, we miss out on special occasions with family. Firefighters understand this is simply part of our job and serving the community, but it is in our meals and time together at the firehouse that we can celebrate. This burger was invented one year when we were working New Year's Eve. We still wanted to be part of the celebration and make our shift a little special, so we tried to make dinner just a bit more glamorous. And yes, a burger can be very glamorous! Serve with a side of Grandpapa's French Fries (see page 168) and you will be celebrating as well.

In a small bowl whisk the mayonnaise with the garlic, lemon juice and Old Bay. Gently fold in the lobster meat to keep nice big chunks and season with salt, pepper and chives.

In a large skillet, cook the bacon over medium heat until crisp. Drain on paper towels and break each strip in half. Reserve the fat.

Light a grill or preheat a grill pan over medium-high heat. Mix all the ground meats together and sprinkle liberally with steak spice, then form into patties. Grill over medium heat until nice char marks are formed on the bottom, about 5 minutes. Flip the burgers and grill for 5 minutes longer. If necessary, finish cooking the burgers on the top rack or over indirect heat to just fully cook through.

Brush the buns with some bacon fat and warm on the grill, in your grill pan or in a 400°F (200°C) oven.

Set the burgers on the bottoms and top with the bacon, lettuce and tomato. Top with a mound of lobster and serve right away.

SERVES 4

½ cup (125 mL) mayonnaise

1 Tbsp (15 mL) fresh garlic, minced

2 Tbsp (30 mL) fresh lemon juice

1 Tbsp (15 mL) Old Bay seasoning

3 lb (1.4 kg) cooked lobster meat

Kosher salt, to taste

Freshly ground pepper, to taste

1 Tbsp (15 mL) chopped fresh chives

8 slices of thick-cut bacon (about ¾ lb/375 g)

1 lb (450 g) ground brisket

1 lb (450 g) ground sirloin

1 lb (450 g) Italian sausage, removed from casing

2 Tbsp (30 mL) steak spice

8 egg buns split

1 cup (250 mL) shredded iceberg lettuce, for garnish

1 tomato, sliced for serving

THE OKTOBERFEST BURGER WITH BEER-BRAISED ONIONS AND APPLES

BEER-BRAISED ONIONS AND APPLES

2 Tbsp (30 mL) butter

2 Tbsp (30 mL) olive oil

2 cups (500 mL) thinly sliced sweet onion

1 cup (250 mL) thinly sliced Granny Smith apples

Kosher salt, to taste

Freshly ground pepper, to taste

2 Tbsp (30 mL) whole grain Dijon mustard

1 tallboy can (16 oz/473 mL) dark lager (Waterloo Dark if available!)

OKTOBERFEST BURGERS

2 lb (900 g) ground heritage pork

2 lb (900 g) bratwurst sausage, removed from casing

1 Tbsp (15 mL) steak spice

1 cup (250 mL) shredded spiced gouda

¼ cup (60 mL) whole grain Dijon mustard

1 cup (250 mL) mayonnaise

8 pretzel rolls, split

1 cup (250 mL) wine sauerkraut, drained

6 large spicy dill pickles, thinly sliced

WE ARE PRETTY proud in Kitchener and Waterloo to have the second largest Bavarian festival outside of Munich, Germany, and it's a big deal around here to our community. It is a time to embrace the region's German heritage and visitors travel from far and wide to join in the festivities—Oktoberfest will always have a special place in my heart especially, as it's where I first laid eyes on my wife! I thought, what better way to thank our community and pay tribute to our local festival of beer, food and the chicken dance, than with an honorary burger. Serve with a batch of my German Potato-Salad Wedges (see page 172) on the side and, of course, a cold Waterloo Dark! *Das ist gut! Prost!*

BEER-BRAISED ONIONS AND APPLES In a large sauté pan over medium-low heat, melt the butter in the olive oil. Add the onion and apples and season liberally with salt and pepper. Toss to coat. Sweat the mixture for about 5 minutes until the onions become soft and translucent. Add the Dijon mustard and mix in well. Turn the heat to medium-high and add the beer. Allow the beer to come to a boil then reduce heat to a simmer. Simmer until the beer has almost completely evaporated, about 20 minutes. Keep warm while you prepare the burgers.

OKTOBERFEST BURGERS Prepare your grill for direct-heat cooking over medium-high heat. Combine the ground pork and bratwurst in a large bowl until well combined. Season the meat mixture with steak spice and form meat into about 6 large patties.

Grill the burgers over high heat for about 4 minutes, rotate 45 degrees then cook 4 minutes longer. Flip the burgers once and grill 4 minutes on the other side. Place the burgers on the top rack of the grill and lower the heat to medium-low. Top each burger with gouda cheese, close the grill lid and finish cooking about 5 minutes longer.

Combine the Dijon and mayonnaise in a small bowl and brush on the buns. Grill or heat the buns just until they become soft.

Assemble the burgers by placing the sauerkraut on the bottom bun. Top with a burger, a heaping spoonful of beer-braised onions and apples and finish with slices of spicy dill pickle and the top bun. Don't forget to grab the napkins!

 SERVES 4–6

ALBERTA BEEF STROGANOFF

JARED WALLACE, COCHRANE FIRE DEPARTMENT, ALBERTA

½ cup (125 mL) unsalted butter, divided

6 oz (170 g) can of sliced mushrooms, drained

2 lb (900 g) beef tenderloin or sirloin steak, cut into ¾-inch (2 cm) strips

2½ cups (625 mL) condensed beef broth, divided

⅓ cup (80 mL) minced onion

¼ cup (60 mL) ketchup

1 tsp (5 mL) garlic salt

⅓ cup (80 mL) all-purpose flour

2 cups (500 mL) sour cream

8-10 oz (225-300 g) uncooked egg noodles

Sitting at the base of Big Hill, in the Bow River Valley and just west of Calgary, Cochrane firefighters are an essential contribution to the healthy culture in their small town. Cochrane has a reputation for its Western culture, which can be felt when one wanders Main Street. Firefighter Jared Wallace offers his recipe for this firehouse and comfort food classic highlighting the pride of Alberta—their beef.

Melt ¼ cup (60 mL) butter in a large skillet. Add mushrooms to the pan and cook for 5 minutes; remove mushrooms.

In the same skillet brown the beef on both sides. Stir in half of the broth with the onion, ketchup and garlic salt and bring to a simmer. Whisk the remaining broth with the flour and add to the meat mixture. Add mushrooms back to the pan and heat to a boil while stirring constantly. Reduce heat to a simmer then stir in sour cream, heating thoroughly.

Cook egg noodles as directed on packaging and drain. Toss with remaining butter. Combine entire dish and mix well, making sure all the noodles are coated in sauce.

 SERVES 6–8

BRUSSELS SPROUT ORECCHIETTE WITH SPICY ITALIAN SAUSAGE

OFTEN DURING WEEKNIGHT shifts at the firehouse we are short on time, but we still love to pull together a great meal and you can always turn to pasta. This dish uses fresh, in-season Brussels sprouts, and resembles a carbonara. It is loaded with spicy and salty flavours and it comes together in a cinch. If you can't find orecchiette pasta try using some bowtie pasta instead.

In a small saucepan simmer the chicken stock until reduced to ¾ cup (190 mL), about 15 minutes.

Bring a large pot of salted water to a boil and add the Brussels sprouts. Cover the pot slightly and cook until Brussels sprouts are crisp-tender, about 5 minutes. Using a slotted spoon, remove the Brussels sprouts and pat them dry. Return the water to a boil and add the orecchiette, cooking until al dente as per package directions. Drain the pasta reserving some of the pasta water.

Meanwhile, in a large, deep skillet, cook the sausage while breaking it up over medium-high heat until well browned and starting to crisp, about 6 minutes. Remove the sausage and drain on paper towels. Add the butter to the skillet and cook over medium-high heat until browned and nutty. Add the Brussels sprouts and almonds and cook until heated through, about 2 minutes. Add the orecchiette along with the reduced chicken stock and simmer, stirring, until the sauce is slightly absorbed, about 2 minutes. Whisk the egg yolks in ½ cup (125 mL) pecorino cheese, season with salt and pepper and add it to the pan mixing well to coat everything. Cook for a few minutes then add the reserved sausage to the pan, tossing well. Taste for seasoning and if not saucy enough add a little of the pasta water. Serve right away garnished with pecorino cheese and freshly ground pepper.

SERVES 4–6

2⅓ cups (580 mL) good-quality chicken stock

1 lb (450 g) Brussels sprouts, halved or quartered (if large)

1 lb (450 g) orecchiette pasta

1 lb (450 g) spicy Italian sausage, removed from casing

¼ cup (60 mL) unsalted butter

½ cup (125 mL) slivered almonds, toasted

2 egg yolks

1 cup (250 mL) finely grated pecorino cheese, divided

Kosher salt, to taste

Freshly ground pepper, to taste

BEEF SHORT RIB SHEPHERD'S PIE

4 beef short ribs
(2¼–2½ lb/1–1.2 kg each)

Kosher salt, to taste

Freshly ground pepper, to taste

2 Tbsp (30 mL) extra virgin
olive oil

1 yellow onion, chopped

2 celery stalks, chopped

6 garlic cloves, crushed

1 carrot, chopped

3⅓ cups (830 mL) dry red wine

3 bay leaves

1 Tbsp (15 mL) fresh thyme

4 cups (1 L) beef broth + more
as needed

1½ lb (700 g) Yukon Gold potatoes, peeled and quartered

¼ cup (60 mL) cream

¼ cup (60 mL) unsalted butter

1 egg yolk, beaten

2 cups (500 mL) peaches
and cream corn kernels
(frozen is okay)

SHEPHERD'S PIE WAS always a comfort food for me and my family growing up. A rich meaty sauce covered in creamy mashed potatoes is something my mom would routinely make for us. As with many of my firehouse recipes this shepherd's pie was created by what was left over in the refrigerator. I guess that's why I had some success on the Food Network's *Chopped Canada*. I took Mom's classic recipe to a new level using my rich and bold short rib ragu as the base. The short rib ragu is a great, versatile recipe on its own, and it can be served over pasta, gnocchi or just about anything that is mashed to soak up all the flavourful juices. But I love the home this ragu has found as the base to this shepherd's pie.

Preheat oven to 350°F (175°C). Season the short ribs with salt and pepper and bring to room temperature.

Heat a large Dutch oven over high heat until hot. Pour in the olive oil and heat until shimmering. Working in batches, sear the ribs on all sides, turning as needed, until well browned. Remove the short ribs and set them aside. Add the onion, celery, garlic and carrot and sauté until veggies begin to caramelize, about 5 minutes. Add the wine, bay leaves and thyme, increase the heat to medium-high and simmer until the wine is reduced by half. Add the broth and bring to a boil. Nestle the ribs back into the Dutch oven and they should be just covered with liquid; add more stock as needed.

Cover the pot, transfer to the oven and cook, adding more broth as needed to maintain the liquid level, until a fork slides easily through the meat, about 2½ hours. Skim any fat off the surface and let the ribs cool in the liquid until they can be handled. Remove the ribs from the pot and pull the meat from the bones discarding the bones. Shred the meat into bite-size pieces and return to the pot.

In a saucepan, cook the potatoes in boiling salted water until tender, about 15 minutes. Drain the potatoes and dry them in the saucepan over low heat. Blitz potatoes in a food processor and place back into the warm pan. In a separate small saucepan, heat the cream and butter until steaming. Pour cream and butter into the potatoes, add the egg yolk and fold to mix well. Season the potatoes with salt and freshly ground pepper.

Increase the oven temperature to 400°F (200°C). Transfer the contents of the Dutch oven to a large baking dish or divide among individual gratin dishes. Cover the top evenly with corn and then with the potatoes and bake until the topping is golden, about 20 minutes.

SERVES 4–6

CAJUN CHICKEN LASAGNA

DARA UZELMAN, MOOSE JAW FIRE DEPARTMENT,
SASKATCHEWAN

1 lb (450 g) lasagna noodles

1 lb (450 g) spicy sausage, cut into small chucks

1 lb (450 g) skinless chicken breasts, cut into small chucks

2 Tbsp (30 mL) Cajun seasoning

1 tsp (5 mL) vegetable oil (optional)

½ cup (125 mL) chopped green onion

½ cup (125 mL) chopped red bell peppers

1 cup (250 mL) chopped mushrooms

2 garlic cloves, minced

3 cups (750 mL) Alfredo Sauce (recipe follows), divided

2 cups (500 mL) shredded mozzarella cheese

ALFREDO SAUCE

3 Tbsp (45 mL) butter

2 Tbsp (30 mL) olive oil

2 garlic cloves, minced

2 cups (500 mL) cream

¼ tsp (1 mL) freshly ground pepper

½ cup (125 mL) grated Parmesan cheese

1 cup (250 mL) grated mozzarella cheese

2 Tbsp (30 mL) chopped fresh flat-leaf parsley

MOOSE JAW ISN'T just home to Mac the Moose and the Snowbirds (Canada's aerobatic air show team). It is also home to 57 firefighters who proudly serve to "Save Lives and Protect Property" in their community and surrounding area. This has been the Moose Jaw Fire Department's motto for over 100 years and its firefighters have never faltered. Firefighter Dara Uzelman knows the importance of keeping his crew well fed and ready for the next alarm and that is evident in his twist on the classic firehouse lasagna.

Preheat oven to 325°F (160°C).

Preboil the lasagna noodles. In a large skillet combine the sausage, chicken and Cajun seasoning and sauté the meat thoroughly—add oil if necessary to keep from sticking. Remove meat from the skillet and set aside. Sauté the onion, peppers, mushrooms and garlic until tender. Remove the veggies from the heat and combine them with the meat and 2 cups (500 mL) Alfredo Sauce.

Lightly grease a 9 × 13–inch (23 × 33 cm) baking dish. Cover the bottom with lasagna noodles. Spread half of the meat/alfredo sauce mixture over top then add another layer of noodles. Top with the remaining Alfredo Sauce then add the last layer of noodles and sprinkle the top layer with mozzarella cheese.

Bake in a preheated oven for 1 hour. Let stand 15 minutes before serving.

ALFREDO SAUCE Melt the butter in a saucepan with olive oil over medium-low heat. Add the garlic and sauté until lightly brown. Add the cream and pepper and bring the mixture to a simmer. Add the Parmesan cheese and simmer for 8 minutes until the sauce thickens. Add the mozzarella cheese and stir until smooth. Stir in the parsley. Enjoy!

SERVE 6–8

CHICKEN AND PEPPER JACK TOSTADAS

Tostadas are the best of both nacho chip and taco. They are fun to build with all the fixin's and in my firehouse you will see some towers! Homemade refried beans and an easy chipotle chicken filling make for a great and easy Mexican feast.

In a bowl mix together the chicken, lime juice, cumin, chipotle, adobo sauce, oil and cilantro. Season to taste with salt and pepper.

To assemble the tostadas preheat the broiler. Spread the refried beans evenly over each tostada and sprinkle with some of the cheese. Transfer to a baking tray and broil until the cheese is lightly browned and just melted, about 1 minute.

Evenly mound the chicken on each tostada and then top with shredded lettuce, Pico de Gallo and a dollop of Avocado Lime Crema. Sprinkle with green onion and cilantro. Serve immediately.

REFRIED BEANS Heat the oil in a large skillet over medium-high heat. Add the onion, coriander and cumin and cook, stirring, until lightly browned, about 2 minutes. Add the garlic and cook, until lightly browned, about 1 minute more. Add the beans and cook, stirring frequently, until thick and amber brown in colour, about 4 minutes. Stir in the salt and pepper to taste.

SERVES 4–6

Meat of 1 rotisserie chicken, shredded (approximately 2 lb/900 g)

⅓ cup (80 mL) freshly squeezed lime juice

1 tsp (5 mL) cumin

1 chipotle pepper in adobo sauce, minced + 1 Tbsp (15 mL) sauce

¼ cup (60 mL) olive oil

¼ cup (60 mL) chopped fresh cilantro

Kosher salt, to taste

Freshly ground pepper, to taste

12 tostada shells

THE FIXIN'S

1 batch Refried Beans (recipe follows)

½ cup (125 mL) grated pepper jack cheese (about 3 oz/90 g)

½ head iceberg lettuce, shredded

1 batch Pico de Gallo (see page 178)

1 batch Avocado Lime Crema (see page 176)

1 green onion, thinly sliced

½ cup (125 mL) fresh cilantro, leaves only

REFRIED BEANS

2 Tbsp (30 mL) olive oil

¼ medium Spanish onion, finely chopped

1 tsp (5 mL) ground coriander

1 tsp (5 mL) ground cumin

4 garlic cloves, minced

15.5 oz (439 mL) can pinto beans (with liquid), mashed

Kosher salt, to taste

Freshly ground pepper, to taste

EGGPLANT PARMESAN

I FOUND THE best way to get my firefighters to eat vegetarian with no grumbling is to simply make it like "dude food." For me this is vegetarian comfort food at its finest. It's all about the Simple Tomato Sauce and melted cheese, and you can put just about anything under there to make a crew happy.

Preheat the oven to 450°F (230°C).

Using some extra virgin olive oil grease a baking tray. Slice each eggplant into 6 pieces about 1–1½ inches (2.5–4 cm) thick. Lightly season each disk with salt and pepper and place on the oiled sheet. Brush the tops with a little more olive oil and bake the eggplant until the slices begin turning deep brown on top, about 12–15 minutes. Remove the eggplants from the oven and set on a plate to cool.

Lower the oven temperature to 350°F (175°C). In an 8 × 12–inch (20 × 30 cm) baking pan, place the largest eggplant slices on the bottom. Over each slice, spread ¼ cup (60 mL) tomato sauce and sprinkle with 1 tsp (5 mL) of basil. Place a slice of mozzarella over each and sprinkle with 1 tsp (5 mL) grated Parmesan cheese. Place the smaller slices of eggplant over each of the disks and repeat with the tomato sauce, basil and the 2 cheeses. Repeat the layering until all the ingredients are used up and finishing with a cheese layer. Sprinkle the toasted bread crumbs and chili flakes over the top of the eggplant dish, and dot with the butter. Bake uncovered until the cheese is melts and the tops turn light brown, about 20 minutes.

SERVES 6

2 Tbsp (30 mL) extra virgin olive oil + more for brushing

2 large eggplants (about 2 lb/ 900 g)

Kosher salt, to taste

Freshly ground pepper, to taste

2 cups (500 mL) Simple Tomato Sauce (see page 180), divided

1 bunch fresh basil leaves, thinly sliced, divided

1 lb (450 g) smoked mozzarella, sliced ⅛ inch (3 mm) thick

½ cup (125 mL) freshly grated Parmesan cheese

¼ cup (60 mL) fresh bread crumbs, lightly toasted

Kosher salt, to taste

Pinch of red chili pepper flakes, to taste

2 Tbsp (30 mL) unsalted butter

FALLIN'-OFF-THE-BONE-ALREADY RIBS

JEFF DERRAUGH AND LAURA DUNCAN, UNITED
FIREFIGHTERS OF WINNIPEG, MANITOBA

¼ cup (60 mL) Fired-Up Santa
Fe Spice (see page 112)

¼ cup (60 mL) brown sugar

2–4 racks baby back ribs (about
1 lb/450 g each)

1 cup (250 mL) of your favourite
barbecue sauce (or try the Five
Star Whisky Barbecue Sauce on
page 112)

AT EVENING SHIFT-change one day, firefighter Laura Duncan started to prepare ribs for her shift's dinner and it led to a group discussion about the best way to cook ribs. Really, there are so many methods that it's ridiculous, and everyone has their tried and true favourite. Boil 'em, braise 'em, bake 'em, barbecue 'em—the list goes on. Laura's way is to season the ribs, wrap them in foil and bake them low and slow before finishing them on the grill. The only problem with this recipe is, as she says, "getting them onto the barbecue without having them fall apart." Yes, Martha, that's a good thing! (Intro by Jeff Derraugh.)

Combine the Fired-Up Santa Fe Spice and brown sugar. Rub the mix on both sides of the ribs and wrap them in cling wrap. I like to let the rub sit on the ribs overnight, or for at least 1 hour, but if time is tight then skip the cling wrap.

Fire up the oven to 300°F (150°C).

Unwrap the ribs. Lay out sheets of foil and spray one side with cooking spray. Wrap the ribs in foil with the meaty side up. Secure all gaps so that the moisture will have a hard time escaping. Ah ha! The secret's revealed.

Place the foil-wrapped racks on a baking tray. Get the ribs into the oven and let them cook for about 2–2½ hours, or until the bones pull back on the ribs about a ¼ inch (6 mm) and the meat is very tender.

Now, fire up the barbecue, and lather the ribs in sauce. Grill them just long enough on each side to get those happy grill marks happening. Give them a quick baste again, and grill them to caramelize the sauce.

If it's cold outside, bake the ribs for 15 minutes more, uncovered, or place under the broiler, but only long enough to give them some colour.

Let the "fall apart" ribs stand for 5 minutes before serving. Slice ribs as necessary into portions or, if it's a firefighter's plate, just go ahead and lay the rack right on it.

This technique works equally well with St. Louis–style spare ribs—in other words, the trimmed rectangular cut of spareribs. Your buddy the butcher will know. In the unlikely event that he doesn't, then pick a rack of spare ribs and instruct the band saw operator to rip 'em right down the middle.

 SERVES 4–8

CHICKEN TACO PIZZA

THIS IS A firefighter's idea of food fusion: tacos and pizza together as one! Being a self-proclaimed connoisseur of both, it only seemed right to take the best of each to create one great dish!

TACO SEASONING Mix all of the ingredients with salt and black pepper in a bowl.

PIZZAS Mix 2 Tbsp (30 mL) taco seasoning and the canola oil in a shallow bowl. Add the chicken to the bowl turning to coat, and marinate for 30 minutes. Preheat the oven to 425°F (220°C) and place your pizza crusts in the oven for about 5 minutes

Preheat a grill or grill pan to medium-high heat. Grill the chicken until cooked through, about 5 minutes per side. Let cool then cut into bite-sized pieces.

Start building your pizza by sprinkling the cheeses on the crusts and top with the chicken. Return the pizzas to the oven, and cook until the cheese is melted and crusts are starting to crisp, about 5 minutes more. Mix the avocado, lime juice, cumin, chili powder, red onion, salt and pepper. When the pizzas are cooked remove them from the oven and top with the avocado mixture, shredded lettuce, Pico de Gallo, crema and cilantro.

SERVES 6

1 Tbsp (15 mL) freshly ground pepper + more to taste

1 batch Pico de Gallo (see page 178)

1 cup (250 mL) shredded iceberg lettuce

½ cup (125 mL) crema (35% sour cream)

¼ cup (60 mL) chopped fresh cilantro

TACO SEASONING

2 Tbsp (30 mL) onion powder

2 Tbsp (30 mL) garlic powder

1 Tbsp (15 mL) chili powder

1 tsp (5 mL) dried oregano

1 tsp (5 mL) cayenne

1 tsp (5 mL) ground cumin

Kosher salt, to taste

Freshly ground pepper, to taste

PIZZAS

¼ cup (60 mL) canola oil + more for brushing

1 lb (450 g) skinless, boneless chicken thighs

2 thin pizza crusts or flatbreads

1 cup (250 mL) shredded smoked mozzarella

1 cup (250 mL) Monterey Jack, shredded

1 avocado

Juice of 1 lime

½ tsp (2 mL) ground cumin

½ tsp (2 mL) chili powder

1 Tbsp (15 mL) diced red onion

1 Tbsp (15 mL) kosher salt + more to taste

EGGS IN HELL

¼ cup (60 mL) extra virgin olive oil

1 cup (250 mL) chopped dry-cured chorizo sausage

1 Spanish onion, coarsely chopped

6 garlic cloves, thinly sliced

1 jalapeño pepper, seeded and diced

1 tsp (5 mL) hot chili flakes

3 cups (750 mL) Simple Tomato Sauce (see page 180)

8 large eggs

Kosher salt, to taste

Freshly ground pepper, to taste

¼ cup (60 mL) finely grated Parmesan cheese

1 loaf of crusty Italian bread, thickly sliced and toasted

FIREFIGHTERS LIKE THE heat, even for breakfast! The "Hell" part of this recipe refers to the spicy tomato sauce that the eggs are poached in.

Heat a cast iron or stainless steel skillet on the stove over medium-high heat and add the olive oil. Add the chorizo, onion, garlic, jalapeño and chili flakes and cook until the vegetables are softened and light brown, about 7 minutes.

Add the tomato sauce and bring to a simmer. Carefully crack the eggs one by one into the sauce and season with salt and pepper.

Cook 5–6 minutes until the whites are set and the yolk is over easy. If you prefer the yolk cooked a little more spoon some of the sauce over and continue cooking for about 3–5 minutes more. Remove from heat and sprinkle the cheese on top. Serve over crusty bread.

SERVES 4

HUNGARIAN GOULASH WITH DUMPLINGS

TREVOR MITCHELL, SARNIA FIRE
DEPARTMENT, ONTARIO

1 Tbsp (15 mL) vegetable oil

1 large onion, finely sliced

1 lb (450 g) veal, chicken or
beef (cook's choice!), chopped

1 tsp (5 mL) paprika

1 red, yellow or orange bell
pepper, chopped

1 celery stalk, chopped

2 tomatoes, chopped

1 bay leaf

2 cloves

Kosher salt, to taste

Freshly ground pepper, to taste

1 Tbsp (15 mL) flour

2 cups (500 mL) water

2 medium potatoes, chopped

1 batch Homemade Dumplings
(recipe follows)

HOMEMADE DUMPLINGS

2 cups (500 mL) all-purpose
flour

¾ cup (190 mL) water

1 egg

1 tsp (5 mL) kosher salt

FIREFIGHTER TREVOR MITCHELL is a proud member of Sarnia Fire Rescue and keeps his crew well fueled. They protect their community not only as firefighters, but also looking after waterways and the CN Tunnel, they offer international aid to the United States and they guard over 20 chemical plants at the mouth of the lower Great Lakes. They also dedicate themselves to Sarnia Lambton by donating their time and have raised over $150,000 for local charities.

In a large cast iron skillet heat the oil over medium heat. Add the onion and brown for about 5 minutes. Add the meat and sprinkle the paprika over top. Add the bell pepper, celery, tomatoes, bay leaf, cloves, salt and pepper. Once the meat draws juice sprinkle everything with flour. Add water and simmer until the meat is cooked and tender, about 2 hours. Add the potatoes in the last half hour of cooking. Serve over the Homemade Dumplings and season to taste with salt and pepper.

HOMEMADE DUMPLINGS In a bowl mix all ingredients until firm. Cut the dough into 1-inch (2.5 cm) squares and using a spoon scrape small pieces into a large pot of boiling salted water. Once the dumplings float they are ready.

 SERVES 4–6

LINGUINE WITH SPICY RED CLAM SAUCE

WE LIKE TO have a well-stocked pantry in the firehouse, and we always keep assorted canned goods, herbs, spices and dry items on hand. That way, when it comes to those busy shifts or long Canadian winter months when fresh isn't available, a fine meal is still in reach. This recipe is budget gourmet at its finest!

Heat a large skillet over medium-low heat and add the olive oil. Add the chili flakes, oregano, thyme and garlic and cook for 1 minute. Stir in the onion and raise the heat to medium, cooking and stirring frequently for about 3–4 minutes. Add the wine and cook until almost all the liquid has evaporated, about 5 minutes. Stir in the clams with their juice, add the tomatoes and cook, keeping a gentle simmer for about 10 minutes. Season the sauce with salt and pepper to taste if needed.

While your sauce is simmering bring a large pot of salted water to a boil. Add the pasta and cook until al dente as per package directions.

Drain the linguine and add it to the clam sauce, tossing it well to coat the noodles. Plate your pasta and garnish it with lots of pecorino cheese, parsley and a little lemon zest.

SERVES 4–6

3 Tbsp (45 mL) extra virgin olive oil

½ tsp (2 mL) red chili pepper flakes

¼ tsp (1 mL) dried oregano leaves

1 tsp (5 mL) dried thyme

6 garlic cloves, slivered

1 onion, finely chopped

½ cup (125 mL) dry red wine

Two 14-oz (410 mL) cans baby clams, in juice

28 oz (796 mL) can crushed tomatoes

Kosher salt, to salt

Freshly ground pepper, to taste

1 lb (450 g) linguine

½ cup (125 mL) grated pecorino cheese, for garnish

½ cup (125 mL) chopped fresh flat-leaf parsley, for garnish

1 tsp (5 mL) grated lemon zest, for garnish

OLD SOUTH CLASSIC FIREHOUSE PULLED PORK

BRIAN BELITSKY, YORKTON FIRE DEPARTMENT, SASKATCHEWAN

1 Tbsp (15 mL) vegetable oil

2 onions, finely chopped

6 garlic cloves, minced

1 Tbsp (15 mL) chili powder

1 tsp (5 mL) freshly ground pepper

1 cup (250 mL) tomato-based chili sauce

¼ cup (60 mL) packed brown sugar

¼ cup (60 mL) cider vinegar

1 Tbsp (15 mL) Worcestershire sauce

1 tsp (5 mL) liquid smoke

1 boneless pork shoulder, trimmed of excess fat (about 3 lb/1.4 kg)

12 kaiser or onion buns, halved and warmed

YORKTON FIREFIGHTERS TAKE great pride in being an important part of the their city, with a growing population of over 18,000 in east-central Saskatchewan. It is a vibrant economic centre for hundreds of thousands of residents in eastern Saskatchewan and western Manitoba. Firefighters truly try to make their city the friendliest, safest and most desirable in which to live, visit and grow.

Firefighter Brian Belitsky has a vital role with the Saskatchewan Professional Firefighters Association. They established the Saskatchewan Professional Firefighters Burn Fund in 1974 as a non-profit registered charity. The main purpose of the charity is to raise and distribute funds to help families of burn patients in Saskatchewan with treatment, care and rehabilitations. All funds raised stay in province with families who need it the most. They have provided the province's two burn units in Regina and Saskatoon with state-of-the-art equipment and the first hyperbaric chamber in Saskatchewan, located in Moose Jaw—an inspiring feat!

Brian Belitsky shares his favourite firehouse creation here. We couldn't have a firefighter-inspired cookbook without a classic pulled pork recipe!

In a skillet heat the oil over medium heat. Add onions and cook until soft, about 5 minutes. Add the garlic, chili powder and pepper and cook, stirring, for 1 minute. Add the chili sauce, brown sugar, vinegar, Worcestershire sauce and liquid smoke. Stir to combine and bring just to a boil. Place pork in a slow cooker and pour sauce over. Cover and cook on low for 10–12 hours or on high for 6 hours, until pork is falling apart. Transfer the pork to a cutting board and pull the meat apart in shreds, using 2 forks. Return to sauce and keep warm. When ready to serve, place the shredded pork in warm buns and spoon sauce over top.

SERVES 6

PAD THAI NOODLES

ROB ANNESLY, MOOSE JAW FIRE DEPARTMENT,
SASKATCHEWAN

MOOSE JAW FIRE Department has no shortage of firehouse chefs. When I reached out to fire departments across Canada looking for their best creations, Moose Jaw firefighters had to have a cook-off to see whose recipe reigned supreme! While friendly competition is commonplace in firehouse kitchens across the country, there was just no need to pick favourites as all the recipes should make Moose Jaw Fire Department and their community very proud. Thanks to firefighter Rob Annesly for this firehouse dish that brings a little exotic touch to the table.

In a large 14-inch (35 cm) deep-fry pan heat olive oil over medium-high heat. Thinly slice the pork and brown for a few minutes, until browned all over. Work in batches if necessary.

Add the Worcestershire sauce along with the garlic, curry powder and allspice and sauté on low to medium-low heat for about 5 minutes. Add the cooking sauces along with jalapeños, stir thoroughly and simmer on low for approximately 20 minutes.

In a large cooking pot bring 1 gallon (4 L) water to a boil. Add rice noodles and allow noodles to cook (be cautious not to overcook noodles), approximately 8–10 minutes or per package directions.

Drain the noodles and add the sauce, stirring thoroughly. Once mixed add the green onion and cilantro. Mix thoroughly and serve with crushed peanuts sprinkled on top.

SERVES 5–6

3 Tbsp (45 mL) olive oil

4 lb (1.8 kg) boneless pork loin chops

2 Tbsp (30 mL) Worcestershire sauce

1 bulb garlic, minced

1 Tbsp (15 mL) curry powder

1 tsp (5 mL) allspice powder

3¼ cups (810 mL) pad Thai cooking sauce (I prefer President's Choice purple label)

1⅔ cups (410 mL) hot pad Thai cooking sauce (I prefer President's Choice red label)

6 medium-sized jalapeños or chili peppers, minced

Four 8.8-oz (250 g) pkgs wide rice noodles

8 green onions, diced (white and green parts)

1 bunch of cilantro, finely chopped

½ cup (125 mL) salted blanched peanuts, crushed (optional)

PENNE WITH MUSHROOMS AND HOT ITALIAN SAUSAGE

BRANDON FIRE DEPARTMENT, MANITOBA

IT IS EASY to understand why Brandon firefighters love this comforting creamy pasta dish with a little heat. If you have ever experienced a Canadian prairie winter then you will know exactly what I mean, and responding to emergency situations when it's 40 below is no winter holiday. This dish is sure to satisfy and warm you from the inside out.

In a large sauté pan, heat olive oil over medium heat. Add the sausage and break it up in the pan while browning it.

Add the onions and mushrooms and sauté for 5–10 minutes, making sure they doesn't stick to the pan and adding a little more oil if necessary.

Add the white wine and scrape the bottom of the pan to get any of the sausage that might have stuck. Reduce the heat to medium-low and add the tomato sauce, tomatoes and bell peppers. Simmer for about 5–10 minutes then add the penne and cream. Cook for another couple of minutes folding everything together. Garnish with green onion and fresh Parmesan.

SERVES 4–6

1 Tbsp (15 mL) olive oil

1 lb (450 g) hot Italian sausage, removed from casing

½ cup (125 mL) diced onions

2 cups (500 mL) sliced mushrooms

½ cup (125 mL) white wine

2 cups (500 mL) tomato sauce

½ cup (125 mL) roma tomatoes, seeded and peeled

¼ cup (60 mL) roasted red bell peppers

2 cups (500 mL) cooked penne al dente, as per pkg directions

¼ cup (60 mL) cream

2 Tbsp (30 mL) chopped green onion

¼ cup (60 mL) fresh Parmesan cheese

SMOKED CHOPS WITH MAPLE BAKED BEANS AND CHEESY ROASTED GARLIC SMASHED POTATOES

KEVIN HARE AND BRIAN BATES, STRATFORD FIRE DEPARTMENT, ONTARIO

MAPLE BAKED BEANS

1 medium onion, peeled

10 garlic cloves

Four 14-oz (398 mL) cans of baked brown beans

2 Tbsp (30 mL) shortening

1 medium onion, chopped finely

2 Tbsp (30 mL) molasses

¼ cup (60 mL) ketchup

¾ cup (190 mL) maple syrup

CHEESY ROASTED GARLIC SMASHED POTATOES

15 Yukon gold potatoes, peeled and chopped

2 bulbs garlic

1 Tbsp (15 mL) olive oil

4 oz (110 g) cream cheese

½ cup (125 mL) warmed milk

Kosher salt, to taste

Freshly ground pepper, to taste

SITUATED ALONG THE Avon River in southwestern Ontario is the beautiful city of Stratford. Firefighters here are ingrained in the community, raising money for local charities and proudly protecting this city best known for its Shakespeare Festival—a fest that draws in hundreds of thousands of visitors each year. This area is also very well known for its local farms, its produce and the products from the surrounding countryside that come together weekly at the famous Stratford Farmers' Market. This is a dream come true for foodies and local chefs alike as Stratford is also home to one of Canada's premier chef schools. It is where firehouse chefs Kevin Hare and Brian Bates went to get inspiration for this locally inspired feast for their hungry crew during a 24-hour shift, which has now become the weekend classic in their firehouse. So whether responding to emergencies, training for combat challenge or volunteering their time to benefit their community, Kevin and Brian make sure their crew operates on a full and happy stomach.

Fire up your barbecue over medium-high heat and preheat your oven to 375°F (190°C).

MAPLE BAKED BEANS Pierce the whole onion with a paring knife 10 times and insert the cloves of garlic into it. Add all ingredients to a large casserole dish, stir and bake for 1 hour. When the beans are finished cooking you can discard the onion.

CHEESY ROASTED GARLIC SMASHED POTATOES For the Cheesy Roasted Garlic Smashed Potatoes, start by cooking the potatoes in a large pot of boiling salted water until tender, about 10–15 minutes. Test with a fork, and when easily pierced go ahead and drain.

Cut off the tops of the garlic bulbs and place in foil. Drizzle with olive oil and bake in the oven until soft and tender and golden brown, about 25 minutes. Let cool and squeeze out the roasted garlic from each clove into a small bowl; set aside.

Add the garlic to the potatoes along with the cream cheese and warmed milk. Start smashing to your desired consistency. Add more milk if necessary and season with salt and pepper.

SMOKED CHOPS Place your chops on the hot grill for about 3 minutes per side, just to get nice grill marks and warm through.

Serve by plating the Smashed Potatoes, smothering them in the Maple Baked Beans and topping it all off with a Smoked Chop—a couple if you're really hungry and have a firefighter's appetite.

SERVES 6–8 + LEFTOVERS FOR SURE!

SMOKED CHOPS

12-16 smoked pork chops from Stratford Farmers' Market (or from your own local market) (about ½ lb/225 g each)

STOVETOP MAC AND CHEESE

1 lb (450 g) elbow macaroni

¼ cup (60 mL) unsalted butter

¼ cup (60 mL) all-purpose flour

4 cups (1 L) whole milk, hot, divided

Kosher salt, to taste

Freshly ground pepper, to taste

1 Tbsp (15 mL) Dijon mustard

¼ tsp (1 mL) cayenne, or to taste

2 cups (500 mL) shredded old cheddar cheese

2 cups (500 mL) shredded smoked mozzarella

¼ cup (60 mL) grated Parmesan cheese

½ lb (225 g) thick-cut bacon, cooked crisp and crumbled

1 Tbsp (15 mL) chopped fresh flat-leaf parsley

EVERYONE, INCLUDING FIREFIGHTERS, loves the iconic little blue box of Kraft mac and cheese. I am sure it brings back childhood memories for most. In fact, I had a captain where it was his favourite meal—no matter what I would suggest for lunch he would always ask for the same thing. He craved it so much that he wanted his last meal before retirement to be his KD and hotdogs! You just can't deny people their ideal comfort food. The blue box will absolutely suffice in a bind, and you will see boxes stashed in firefighters' lockers, but homemade mac and cheese always reigns supreme. Use any variety of cheese you like to give this stovetop method a new taste each time. Don't forget to make a double batch for the Mac and Cheese Croquettes (see page 13)!

Bring a large pot of salted water to a boil. Add the pasta and cook al dente according to the package directions, about 6 minutes. Drain, rinse and set aside.

In a heavy saucepan or extra-large skillet set over medium-high heat, melt the butter. Whisk in the flour and cook, whisking constantly until the roux cooks and bubbles a bit, about 2 minutes. Slowly pour in 3 cups (750 mL) hot milk and cook, whisking constantly until the sauce thickens, about 5 minutes. Season the sauce to taste with salt and pepper. Bring the sauce just to a boil then reduce the heat to low and cook stirring for 2 minutes. Stir in the Dijon and cayenne and then gradually add the cheddar and smoked mozzarella cheeses one handful at a time, stirring constantly until all of the cheese has melted into the sauce. Stir in the remaining 1 cup (250 mL) milk. Add the cooked pasta to the sauce and stir to coat. Taste mac and cheese and season to taste one more time with salt and pepper.

Transfer to a serving dish and sprinkle the top with the Parmesan cheese, bacon and parsley. Serve immediately and enjoy!

SERVES 4

STUFFED SPAGHETTI SQUASH
WITH STRAWBERRY SPINACH SALAD

PAUL BUSSE, MOOSE JAW FIRE DEPARTMENT, SASKATCHEWAN

FIREFIGHTER PAUL BUSSE, who is another proud Moose Jaw firehouse chef, transforms spaghetti squash into a delicious carrier for his amazing meat and vegetable sauce. Melt some cheese on top and it doesn't get much more comforting than that! He serves it alongside his Strawberry Spinach Salad to round out the meal and keep his brothers and sisters strong and ready for the shift ahead.

Start by preheating your oven to 400°F (200°C).

You can put the squash in plain, or you can do a variation where you rub the squash with butter or olive oil, then sprinkle with brown sugar or a pinch of salt and pepper before baking with the sauce.

Bake for 1 hour or until squash is tender and pulls apart easily. I start preparing the sauce as soon as the squash goes into the oven.

Brown the ground beef and Italian sausage with the onion, garlic and season with 1 Tbsp (15 mL) salt and 1 Tbsp (15 mL) pepper. Drain if needed.

Add the mushrooms, zucchini, red and green peppers, sauce, basil, oregano, Italian seasoning, fennel and sugar.

Simmer for at least 1 hour. Once the sauce is ready and the squash is cooked, ladle the sauce into the squash and sprinkle with mozzerella. Put the squash back into the oven to melt the cheese, roughly 5–10 minutes. You can sprinkle with additional Parmesan cheese for added flavour. Serve with the Strawberry Spinach Salad (recipe follows).

STRAWBERRY SPINACH SALAD Toss all ingredients together and serve.

SERVES 10

STRAWBERRY SPINACH SALAD

1½ lb (700 g) strawberries, sliced

3 cups (750 mL) baby spinach

1 cup (250 mL) chopped pecans

1 cup (250 mL) dried cranberries

1½ cups (375 mL) thin sliced red onion

1 cup (250 mL) crumbled feta cheese

½ cup (125 mL) store-bought raspberry vinaigrette dressing, or to taste

5 spaghetti squash, halved and seeded (about 4 lb/1.8 kg each)

2 Tbsp (30 mL) butter (optional)

2 Tbsp (30 mL) olive oil (optional)

2 Tbsp (30 mL) brown sugar (optional)

1 Tbsp (15 mL) kosher salt + a pinch for the variation (optional)

1 Tbsp (15 mL) freshly ground black pepper + more to taste

4 lb (1.8 kg) lean or extra lean ground beef

1½ lb (700 g) ground Italian sausage, removed from casing

1 large onion

7 garlic cloves (more to taste), minced

3 cups (750 mL) mushrooms

1 zucchini, chopped

1 red bell pepper, chopped

1 green bell pepper, chopped

1 cup (250 mL) pasta sauce

1 Tbsp (15 mL) dried basil

1 Tbsp (15 mL) dried oregano

1 Tbsp (15 mL) Italian seasoning

1 tsp (5 mL) ground fennel

2 Tbsp (30 mL) sugar

2 cups (500 mL) grated mozzarella cheese

¼ cup (60 mL) grated Parmesan cheese (optional)

SWEET AND SMOKY MEATLOAF

RETIRED FIRE CHIEF JOHN DEHOOGE,
OTTAWA FIRE SERVICES, ONTARIO

2 lb (900 g) ground beef chuck

1 cup (250 mL) finely grated Parmesan cheese

¾ cup (190 mL) plain dry bread crumbs

½ cup (125 mL) ketchup + more for serving

½ medium onion, coarsely grated

1 garlic clove, minced

2 large eggs, beaten

2 Tbsp (30 mL) brown sugar

½ tsp (2 mL) kosher salt

½ tsp (2 mL) freshly ground black pepper

5-7 slices smoked bacon

Everyone has that one particular dish that they associate with comfort food, and for the former Fire Chief of our nation's capital this is it! Now serving as an Executive for the International Association of Fire Chiefs, John is a passionate voice for the fire service and he brings that same fire into his kitchen.

Position a rack in the middle of the oven and preheat to 400°F (200°C).

In a large bowl, crumble the ground beef. Add the cheese, bread crumbs, ketchup, onion, garlic, eggs, brown sugar, salt and pepper. Using your hands, gently mix to combine.

Transfer the meat mixture to a 9 × 13–inch (23 × 33 cm) baking dish and form into a roughly 5 × 12–inch (12 × 30 cm) meatloaf. Drape the bacon slices diagonally over the top and sides of the meatloaf and bake until the bacon is browned and the meatloaf gives slightly when pressed in the centre, about 45 minutes.

Let the meatloaf stand about 10 minutes before slicing and serving.

 SERVES 6

SPAGHETTI SQUASH CARBONARA

I**F YOU STRUGGLE** with gluten intolerance that doesn't mean you need to totally give up your favourite pasta dishes. Replacing pasta noodles with spaghetti squash gives you a healthy and very tasty alternative, and it gives this carbonara a little lightness, texture and crunch.

Preheat the oven to 375°F (190°C). Sprinkle the bottom of a large, shallow baking dish with 1 tsp (5 mL) salt and ¾ tsp (4 mL) pepper. Place the squash flesh side down in the pan and add enough water to come up about ¼ inch (6 mm). Cover tightly with foil and cook in the oven until the squash is just fork tender, about 1–1½ hours. Shred the squash with a fork and transfer to a large heatproof bowl.

In a large sauté pan over medium heat, cook the pancetta until it starts to become crispy, about 5 minutes. Pour off some fat, if necessary, and then add the shallots and garlic. Sauté for 1 minute until the garlic and shallots are fragrant and begin to caramelize. Add the white wine and cook until the liquid has completely evaporated, about 5 minutes.

In a medium bowl whisk the yolks and whole egg together with the cheese and the parsley and season with the remaining salt and pepper; set aside. Add the spaghetti squash to the pan and toss to thoroughly combine with the bacon mixture. Turn heat to low then add the egg-cheese mixture. Toss well to coat—the heat from the squash should cook the eggs through but still keep them nice and creamy. Season with salt and lots of pepper and serve immediately.

SERVES 4–6

2 tsp (10 mL) kosher salt + more for serving, divided

1¼ tsp (6 mL) freshly ground pepper + more for serving, divided

1 large spaghetti squash (about 2 lb/900 g), halved and seeded

½ lb (225 g) pancetta, diced

2 Tbsp (30 mL) minced shallots

2 tsp (10 mL) minced garlic

¼ cup (60 mL) white wine

2 egg yolks + 1 whole egg

1 cup (250 mL) freshly grated Parmesan cheese

2 Tbsp (30 mL) chopped fresh flat-leaf parsley

THAI DRUNKEN NOODLES

I F YOU LOVE fried noodles then give this Bangkok street food a try. The "Drunken" part could refer to the sake used in the sauce, but I think it actually refers to the likelihood of consuming a few cold beers while eating to tame the spice!

Pour boiling water over noodles in a large bowl and set aside for 5 minutes (or as per packet instructions), then drain when ready. Make sure to rinse noodles under cold water.

Heat the oil in a wok or large pan over high heat. Add garlic and chilies and cook for 10 seconds until fragrant. Add the eggs and cook, stirring constantly until just set. Add the chicken and fry until browned and cooked partially through, about 4 minutes.

Add the shallots, green onions and about 1 Tbsp (15 mL) Thai Drunken Sauce and stir-fry for 30 seconds, just to coat the chicken. Add the noodles and the rest of the sauce and cook for a couple minutes until the sauce has coated the noodles completely and they start to brown.

Remove from heat and add the basil and tomatoes, stirring until they are mixed in well. Serve immediately with a cold Thai beer!

THAI DRUNKEN SAUCE Put all the ingredients into a small bowl and mix together.

SERVES 4

14 oz (400 g) pkg pad Thai noodles

2 Tbsp (30 mL) peanut oil

3 large cloves of garlic, minced

3 Thai bird's eye chilies, finely chopped, seeds included (that's the hot part!)

2 eggs, beaten

4 boneless chicken thighs (about ¼ lb/125 g each), cut into bite-sized pieces

2 shallots, chopped

2 green onions, white and green part chopped

1 batch Thai Drunken Sauce (recipe follows), divided

1 cup (250 mL) Thai basil

½ cup (125 mL) cherry tomatoes, halved

THAI DRUNKEN SAUCE

3 Tbsp (45 mL) oyster sauce

2 Tbsp (30 mL) mushroom soy sauce

2 Tbsp (30 mL) dark soy sauce

2 tsp (10 mL) sugar

½ cup (125 mL) sake (rice wine)

FIVE STAR WHISKY BRISKET

JEFF DERRAUGH, UNITED FIREFIGHTERS OF WINNIPEG, MANITOBA

FIRED-UP SANTA FE SPICE

2 Tbsp (30 mL) paprika
(sweet if possible)

2 Tbsp (30 mL) chili powder

2 Tbsp (30 mL) kosher salt

1 Tbsp (15 mL) granulated garlic
(roasted if you have it)

1 Tbsp (15 mL) cayenne

1 Tbsp (15 mL) ground
coriander

1 Tbsp (15 mL) dried oregano

2 tsp (10 mL) ground cumin

2 tsp (10 mL) freshly
ground pepper

BRISKET

¾ cup (190 mL) brown sugar

1 beef brisket (about 5-6 lb
/2.2-2.7 kg)

2 Tbsp (30 mL) liquid smoke

Five Star Whisky BBQ Sauce,
to taste (recipe follows)

FIVE STAR WHISKY BBQ SAUCE

3 cups (750 mL) ketchup

1 cup (250 mL) Canadian
whisky

½ cup (125 mL) honey

⅓ cup (80 mL) brown sugar

¼ cup (60 mL) molasses

1 Tbsp (15 mL) dried oregano

1 tsp (5 mL) red chili pepper
flakes (or more if you like it hot)

As a bonus to this brisket recipe, you get my favourite BBQ sauce recipe, which stars a big old cup of whisky. This sauce goes great on ribs or chicken or, as I originally tasted it, as a meatball sauce. It's got great zip! This brisket gets its title not only from the Five Star whisky being used in the sauce, but because the sauce also rates five stars. It is a firehouse favourite! One of the golden rules of firehouse cooking is of course making sure everything tastes great (or you'll hear about it), but also keeping meals inexpensive for your crew. However, if quality is going to trump budget, Crown Royal is distilled an hour north of Winnipeg in Gimli, so replace the Five Star whisky and go for the bottle in the little purple bag. (Intro by Jeff Derraugh.)

FIRED-UP SANTA FE SPICE Simply combine all of the above together and store in a spice jar.

BRISKET Mix Fired-Up Santa Fe Spice with brown sugar and spread it over both sides of the brisket. Allow the brisket to sit out for 1 hour at room temperature. Place it in a roaster, and drizzle liquid smoke over top.

Warm the oven to 200°F (95°C). We want a low, slow roast.

Cover the roaster, and place in the oven for approximately 1 hour 10 minutes per pound. I usually bake a 6 lb (2.7 kg) brisket for 7 hours before finishing with sauce. The brisket will cook unattended in its own juices.

Drain about two-thirds of the liquid off the brisket, top it with a healthy helping of BBQ sauce, and bake a further hour to warm through.

Uncover roaster and broil top of brisket to caramelize the sauce.

Let the brisket cool for 10 minutes. Slice it against the grain, fan out strips of brisket on plate and top with the warmed BBQ sauce.

If you managed to restrain everyone and actually have leftovers, cook them up in the sauce the next day and serve on toasted buns.

FIVE STAR WHISKY BBQ SAUCE Blend the Five Star Whisky BBQ Sauce ingredients together in a saucepan and keep warm.

SERVES 6–8 + LEFTOVERS

BAKED MUSSELS WITH SEAFOOD PASTA

RICK HISCOCK, LABRADOR CITY FIRE DEPARTMENT, NEWFOUNDLAND

LABRADOR CITY WAS built around the rich iron ore deposits of the area and it became known as the "Land of the Hard-working People." Sitting on the Quebec border, the Labrador City firefighters maintain that motto as they protect and serve their community with just six full-time firefighters who are assisted by 28 dedicated volunteers to assist them when in need. When I asked firefighter Rick Hiscock to describe his locally inspired firehouse creation to me, this is what he said (translation accompanied!): "We's [us] Newfies [Newfoundlanders] likes de sea food and dis ones some shockin' good [is very likeable]!" I couldn't agree more Rick.

Preheat your oven to 450°F (230°C). Place mussels on a baking tray and sprinkle liberally with freshly ground pepper. Place tray in the oven and cook for approximately 12 minutes until all or most of the mussels have opened. Discard any that remain closed.

SEAFOOD PASTA Set a large sauté pan over medium heat and add the olive oil. Once oil begins to simmer add the garlic and cook until fragrant, about 30 seconds. Working in batches, sauté the shrimp and scallops until almost cooked through—just a couple minutes per side—then remove them to a plate. Now add the vegetables to the pan and sauté until softened, about 5 minutes. Add the baby clams and all the reserved shrimp and scallops to the pan. Pour the alfredo sauce over top and bring to a simmer.

In a small bowl combine the reserved clam juice, oyster sauce and corn starch. Whisk together well and add to the pan. Once sauce thickens to desired consistency add your cooked linguine to the pan and toss well to make sure all the noodles are good and coated with the sauce. Add a little pasta-cooking water if the pasta sauce gets too thick.

Load Seafood Pasta onto a plate and top with grated Parmesan cheese and ground pepper. Arrange baked mussels around the plate. Serve to your gut founderin' guests!

SERVES 4–6 GUESTS

1 lb (450 g) fresh mussels, scrubbed and debearded

Freshly ground pepper, to taste

SEAFOOD PASTA

1 Tbsp (15 mL) olive oil

1 Tbsp (15 mL) fresh garlic, minced

1 lb (450 g) large shrimp, cleaned and deveined

1 lb (450 g) fresh sea scallops

2 celery stalks, chopped

½ lb (225 g) button mushrooms, halved

2 mixed bell peppers, chopped

14 oz (398 mL) can baby clams, drained and juice reserved

3¼ cups (810 mL) jar alfredo sauce

1 Tbsp (15 mL) oyster sauce

1 Tbsp (15 mL) corn starch

1 lb (450 g) linguine, cooked, cooking water reserved

Kosher salt, to taste

½ cup (125 mL) fresh grated Parmesan cheese, for garnish

Freshly ground pepper, to taste

CARNE ASADA AND GRILLED VEGGIES WITH CHIMICHURRI SAUCE

STEAK

3 bulbs garlic, roughly chopped

¾ cup (190 mL) freshly squeezed lime juice

¼ cup (60 mL) freshly squeezed orange juice

¼ cup (60 mL) silver tequila

¼ cup (60 mL) soy sauce

1 bunch roughly chopped fresh cilantro

1 jalapeño, diced

1 tsp (5 mL) cumin powder

1 tsp (5 mL) smoked paprika

1 Tbsp (15 mL) freshly cracked black pepper

1½–2 lb (700 g–900 g) skirt steak or flank steak

1 batch Chimichurri Sauce, for serving (see page 176)

GRILLED VEGGIES

3 red bell peppers, seeded and halved

3 sweet potatoes (about 1 lb/450 g), sliced lengthwise into ¼-inch (6 mm) thick rounds

3 zucchini, sliced lengthwise into ½-inch (1 cm) thick rectangles

12 cremini mushrooms

1 lb (450 g) asparagus, trimmed

12 green onions, trimmed

12 small tomatoes

¼ cup (60 mL) grapeseed oil

THERE WAS A time when I first introduced my chimichurri sauce to the firehouse that I would receive weekly phone calls or text messages during all hours asking, "How do I make that chimi sauce again?" Anything to help a brother out! In this recipe, highly seasoned steak is sliced thin and sits on top a bed of grilled veggies. This is a perfect summertime main course with the entire dish being prepared on the grill. The Chimichurri Sauce adds the perfect balance of colour, brightness and zip to this and just about any dish.

STEAK Combine the garlic, lime juice, orange juice, tequila, soy sauce, cilantro, jalapeño, cumin, paprika and pepper in a resealable plastic bag. Add the steak and marinate in the refrigerator for 2 hours. Remove from refrigerator and let marinate at room temperature another 30–45 minutes.

Heat your grill over medium-high heat. Place the steak on the hot grill and cook for 4 minutes, turn 180 degrees and cook for 3 minutes longer. Flip the steak over and finish cooking for 3–5 minutes, depending on desired doneness and thickness. Remove from the grill to a cutting board and let rest lightly tented with foil for 10 minutes. In the meantime grill your veggies.

GRILLED VEGGIES Brush or toss the vegetables with the grapeseed oil to coat lightly. Sprinkle the vegetables liberally with salt and pepper. Working in batches, grill the vegetables directly on the grill until tender and lightly charred all over, about 8–10 minutes for the sweet potatoes; 7 minutes for the peppers, zucchini and mushrooms; 4 minutes for the asparagus, green onions and tomatoes. The key to getting those great grill marks is to not shift the vegetables too frequently once they've been placed on the hot grill. Place vegetables on a large platter. Slice the flank steak across the grain and lay on top of the vegetables. Drizzle the entire platter with Chimichurri Sauce and enjoy!

SERVES 4–6

Kosher salt, to taste

Freshly ground pepper, to taste

CAULIFLOWER STEAKS
WITH SALSA VERDE

TELLING FIREFIGHTERS THAT they are having steak for dinner and then serving cauliflower can be putting your own life at risk! Luckily when I served this cooler heads prevailed and, once they let flavour do the talking, it won them over. Serve these steaks as a side dish or in place of beef for a healthy vegetarian option for your crew. This recipe is another great example of how vegetables can be "dude food."

SALSA VERDE To make the salsa verde, in a large bowl, whisk the parsley with the cilantro, tarragon, capers, pickles, garlic, mustards and olive oil. Set aside.

CAULIFLOWER STEAKS Cut the cauliflower from top to bottom into four ½-inch (1 cm) thick steaks and season them liberally with salt and pepper. In a large skillet, heat the grapeseed oil until very hot. Add the cauliflower in a single layer and cook over high heat until well browned. Carefully turn the steaks, add the wine and cook until it has evaporated and the cauliflower is easily pierced with a knife, 3–5 minutes.

Transfer each cauliflower steak to a platter and sprinkle with the lemon zest. Stir the lemon juice and vinegar into your salsa verde and season with salt and pepper. Spoon the sauce on the cauliflower steak and serve. Enjoy!

SERVES 4

SALSA VERDE

¼ cup (60 mL) chopped flat-leaf parsley

2 Tbsp (30 mL) chopped cilantro

2 Tbsp (30 mL) chopped tarragon

1½ Tbsp (23 mL) capers, drained and coarsely chopped

6 zesty baby dill pickles, chopped

1 garlic clove, grated

1 Tbsp (15 mL) Dijon mustard

1 Tbsp (15 mL) grainy mustard

⅓ cup (80 mL) extra virgin olive oil

CAULIFLOWER STEAKS

1 large head of cauliflower

Kosher salt, to taste

Freshly ground pepper, to taste

2 Tbsp (30 mL) grapeseed oil

½ cup (125 mL) dry white wine

½ tsp (2 mL) finely grated lemon zest

4½ Tbsp (67.5 mL) fresh lemon juice

1 tsp (5 mL) red wine vinegar

CAST IRON HANGER STEAK WITH DIJON CREAM SAUCE

1 lb (450 g) hanger steak, trimmed of excess fat and tissue

Kosher salt, to taste

Freshly ground pepper, to taste

1 Tbsp (15 mL) unsalted butter

1 Tbsp (15 mL) olive oil

5 Tbsp (75 mL) cognac or brandy, divided

¼ cup (60 mL) heavy cream

2 Tbsp (30 mL) Dijon mustard

1 Tbsp (15 mL) minced flat-leaf parsley

MY GRANDPAPA WAS a Quebec City firefighter and my inspiration to become one ever since I was a very young boy. I wanted to be a firefighter just like him. Little did I know I was also following in his footsteps as a firehouse chef! This was his favourite way of cooking a steak: a quick fry in a cast iron pan with an amazing pan sauce. Hanger steak is not your typical cut but once you discover it you will be in love with its robust beef flavour; it is available at any good butcher. In order to get the best out of this recipe, a cast iron pan is a must and it is one of my preferred ways to cook. If you don't already have one stashed away in a cupboard or attic somewhere then it's time to get one. You can cook with it from the stovetop or inside the oven, and achieve a perfect sear with precision heat. With just a little maintenance a good cast iron pan will last you a lifetime.

Season the steaks liberally with salt and pepper. Melt the butter in the oil in a large cast iron skillet over medium-high heat. Once the pan begins to smoke add the steaks. Cook, turning just once, about 3 minutes per side depending on the thickness, or until an instant read thermometer reads 130°F (54°C) in the thickest part. Remove pan from heat and transfer steaks to a cutting board and loosely tent with foil.

Add 4 Tbsp (60 mL) liquor to the pan and stir, scraping any browned bits from the bottom with a wooden spoon. Return pan to medium-high heat and cook for about 20 seconds. Add cream and mustard, season with salt and pepper and cook, stirring vigorously until the sauce just comes together. Stir in remaining liquor and keep warm over low heat. Slice the hanger steaks across the grain in ¼-inch (6 mm) pieces and drizzle sauce over top. Serve steaks garnished with parsley and black pepper.

SERVES 4

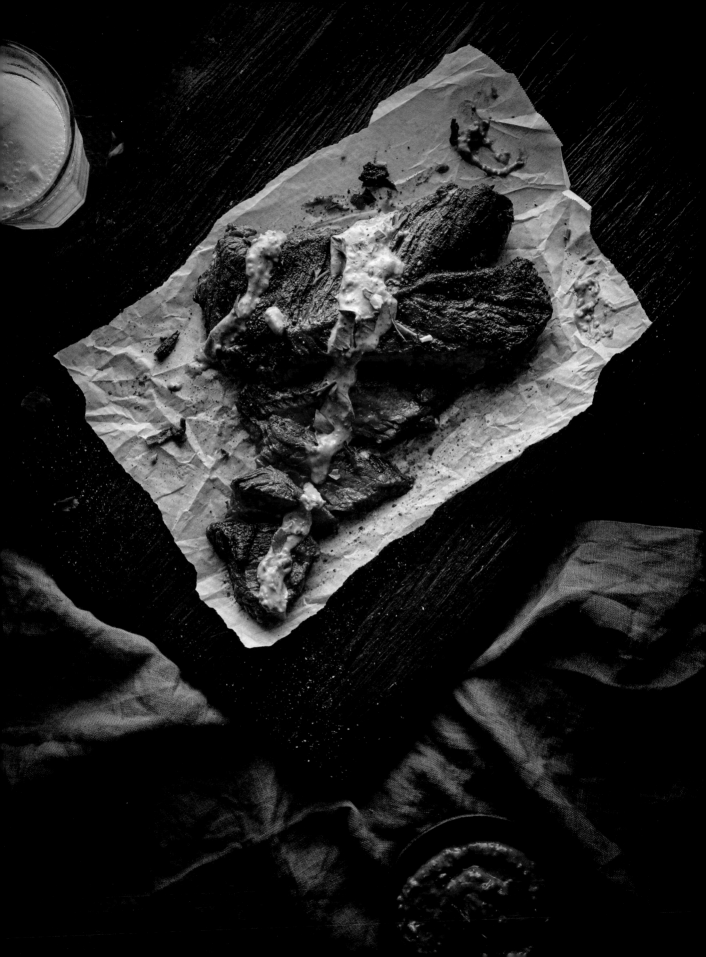

CRANBERRY MEATBALLS AND RICE WITH GARLIC PARMESAN ASPARAGUS

GORD HEWITT, MOOSE JAW FIRE DEPARTMENT, SASKATCHEWAN

2 large eggs

¼ cup (60 mL) soy sauce

1 cup (250 mL) finely chopped onion

4 garlic cloves, minced (adjust to taste)

2 tsp (10 mL) kosher salt

1 tsp (5 mL) fresh cracked pepper

4 lb (1.8 kg) lean ground beef

5⅔ cups (1.4 L) cranberry sauce

2 cups (500 mL) chili sauce

2 cups (500 mL) ketchup

½ cup (125 mL) brown sugar

¼ cup (60 mL) white vinegar

4 cups (1 L) whole grain brown rice

GARLIC PARMESAN ASPARAGUS

1 lb (450 g) asparagus

2 Tbsp (30 mL) extra virgin olive oil

2 Tbsp (30 mL) grated Parmesan cheese

4 cloves garlic, minced

GORD IS CURRENTLY the proud president of the Moose Jaw Firefighters Association. He leads his fellow firefighters in tough battles on and off the fireground. His association helped secure the lone hyperbaric chamber between Edmonton and Toronto, pledged financial support to help keep it local and also raised thousands of dollars for local charities within the city of Moose Jaw and for the Saskatchewan Professional Firefighters Burn Fund. He knows the importance that cooking has within our firehouses to build camaraderie and a strong team. Enjoy Gord's unique and delicious firehouse creation!

Preheat the oven to 350°F (175°C).

Mix the eggs, soy sauce, onion, garlic, salt and pepper together in a large bowl. Add the ground beef and mix well. Shape into approximately 2-inch (5 cm) meatballs

Brown the meatballs in a large frying pan over medium-high heat and place in a large casserole dish.

Mix the cranberry sauce, chili sauce, ketchup, brown sugar and vinegar together in a large bowl. Pour the sauce over the meatballs and bake uncovered in the oven for approximately 45 minutes.

Cook the rice according to package directions. While the rice and meatballs are cooking, assemble the asparagus.

GARLIC PARMESAN ASPARAGUS Snap the woody ends off the asparagus and place on a baking tray. Cover lightly with oil and mix asparagus around so it gets lightly covered with the oil. Sprinkle with Parmesan cheese and garlic. Bake for 15 minutes in oven.

ASSEMBLY When the meatballs are done, place cooked rice on a plate and cover with meatballs and sauce so there is enough sauce to soak into all the rice. Serve garnished with Garlic Parmesan Asparagus.

 SERVES 6

DUCK AU POIVRE
WITH PARSLEY SALAD

I LOVE INTRODUCING new tastes and ingredients in the firehouse. When I first started as a rookie our meals were quite ordinary and consisted mostly of chilis, stews, sausages and sauerkraut, basic spaghetti and burgers. All these meals are part of a tradition that I love, and they still have their place on our firehouse menus today. Having the ability to offer new experiences and tastes and to make people happy through food is where I find the most joy in cooking. This elegant duck dish is a perfect example as it is a simple take on the French bistro classic.

Using a sharp knife trim any excess fat from the edges of the duck. Pat the duck completely dry with paper towels. Place the duck, skin side up, on a cutting board. Score the skin with the tip of a knife by making shallow diagonal cuts ½ inch (1 cm) apart in one direction, then repeating in the other direction, creating a diamond pattern. Season both sides of the duck liberally with the salt. Place the garlic on a cutting board and sprinkle with another pinch of salt. With the backside of your knife mash the garlic and salt into a paste. Massage the duck with the garlic paste (again on both sides), then press the pepper evenly onto the surface (again on both sides). Set aside for at least 1 hour at room temperature.

Heat a cast iron skillet over medium-high heat until hot but not smoking. Carefully add the duck breast skin-side down, and let it sizzle for several minutes. Using tongs, check to see that the skin is not browning too quickly and that the garlic is not burning. Cook until the duck skin is golden and crisp, 6–7 minutes. Turn the duck breast over and cook for 4 minutes more. Transfer the duck to a carving board and let rest for at least 10 minutes. Deglaze the pan with some red wine, scraping up all the browned bits, simmer for about 5 minutes then reduce heat to low, add the butter and keep the sauce warm.

Cut the duck at an angle into ¼-inch (6 mm) thick slices and arrange on a platter. Drizzle the duck with pan juice and top with a fluffy pile of parsley salad. Serve immediately and enjoy!

PARSLEY SALAD In a small bowl, whisk together the lemon juice, salt, pepper, garlic and oil. Dress the parsley lightly with the dressing and then fold in the Parmesan shavings.

2 Muscovy duck breasts (about 1 lb/450 g each)

Kosher salt, to taste

4 garlic cloves, minced

1 Tbsp (15 mL) freshly ground pepper + more to taste

¼ cup (60 mL) good-quality red wine

1 Tbsp (15 mL) unsalted butter

PARSLEY SALAD

2 cups (500 mL) loosely packed flat-leaf parsley

2 tsp (10 mL) freshly squeezed lemon juice

Kosher salt, to taste

1 small garlic clove, minced

2 Tbsp (30 mL) extra virgin olive oil

¼ cup (60 mL) shaved Parmesan cheese

 SERVES 4

CRISP BRAISED DUCK LEGS WITH APRICOTS AND BRANDY

AFTER SO MANY chicken dishes in the firehouse you sometimes just have to try something different! Try this braised dish that creates fall-off-the-bone tender duck legs. It has a very simple preparation, yet it will seem like an elegant weekend dinner for family, whether it is served at home or in the firehouse.

Season the duck legs liberally with salt and pepper. Melt the butter in the oil in a Dutch oven or other heavy-duty pot over medium-high heat. Working in batches, put the duck legs in the pot skin-side down and cook until the skin is very well browned and crisp, about 10 minutes (reduce the heat to medium if they brown too fast). Flip duck legs once and cook a couple minutes on the other side. Transfer legs to a plate and drain off all but 2 Tbsp (30 mL) fat from the pot, saving the remaining drained fat for another day.

Add the carrots, celery, onion and garlic to the pot and cook over medium heat, stirring often until the garlic is just starting to turn golden-brown, 3–4 minutes. Stir in the apricots, thyme and brandy. Arrange the duck legs skin-side up on top of the vegetables and add enough chicken broth to cover the duck by about ½ inch (1 cm), up to 8 cups (2 L). Increase the heat to high and bring the liquid to a boil. Add salt and pepper to taste, reduce the heat to low, cover the pot and cook until fork tender, 1½–2 hours. Turn off the heat and let the duck rest in the juice for 15–30 minutes. Skim off any fat from the surface of the sauce.

With a slotted spoon, distribute the vegetables among a platter. Top with the duck legs. Stir another dash of brandy into the sauce in the pot, then drizzle the sauce over the duck legs. Garnish with chopped parsley and serve.

SERVES 6

Six ¾–1 lb (375–450 g) fresh duck legs, trimmed of excess fat

Kosher salt, to taste

Freshly ground pepper, to taste

1 Tbsp (15 mL) grapeseed oil

1 Tbsp (15 mL) butter

4 carrots, cut into 1-inch (2.5 cm) pieces

2 celery stalks, cut into 1-inch (2.5 cm) pieces

1 yellow onion, chopped

6 garlic cloves, minced

1 lb (450 g) dried apricots, thinly sliced

4 sprigs fresh thyme

3 Tbsp (45 mL) brandy + extra dash for the sauce

4–8 cups (1–2 L) good-quality chicken stock

2 Tbsp (30 mL) finely chopped fresh flat-leaf parsley, for garnish

GRILLED AHI TUNA WITH SICILIAN SALSA

AHI TUNA COULD very well be my favourite ingredient both to cook and to eat. During my appearance on Season 2 of the Food Network's *Chopped Canada* you can only imagine my giant sigh of relief when I saw a beautiful piece of tuna as one of my secret ingredients in the main course round! This dense, firm-fleshed fish is absolutely perfect for grilling and absorbs rubs and marinades wonderfully. Cooking it rare will ensure its maximum tenderness and flavour, and the Sicilian Salsa is a perfect briny compliment to this or any grilled fish.

Prepare a grill for direct grilling over high heat and oil the grill rack. Coat the tuna with grapeseed oil.

SPICE RUB In a small bowl mix together the garlic powder, basil, fennel seeds, chili flakes, salt and pepper. Sprinkle both sides of each tuna steak generously with the spice rub.

SICILIAN SALSA To make the salsa, combine all ingredients in a bowl, taste and season with salt. Set aside.

Grill the tuna directly over high heat for 1–2 minutes per side, until grill-marked and still rare in the middle. Arrange the tuna steaks on individual plates and top with the salsa. Serve alongside your favourite pasta.

SERVES 4–6

4 ahi tuna steaks (about ½ lb/225 g each)

2 Tbsp (30 mL) grapeseed oil, for coating

SPICE RUB

1 Tbsp (15 mL) garlic powder

1 Tbsp (15 mL) dried basil

1 tsp (5 mL) ground fennel seeds

¼ tsp (1 mL) red chili pepper flakes

½ Tbsp (7.5 mL) kosher salt

1 tsp (5 mL) lemon pepper or freshly ground black pepper

SICILIAN SALSA

¼ cup (60 mL) chopped cured black olives

1 cup (250 mL) chopped tomatoes

¼ cup (60 mL) chopped fresh basil

3 garlic cloves, minced

¼ tsp (1 mL) cayenne

2 Tbsp (30 mL) extra virgin olive oil

Juice of ½ lemon

Kosher salt, to taste

LEMON-BREADED RACK OF PORK

3½ lb (1.6 kg) six-rib bone-in pork loin roast

1 Tbsp (15 mL) extra virgin olive oil

Kosher salt, to taste

Freshly ground pepper, to taste

2 cups (500 mL) loosely packed flat-leaf parsley leaves

3 garlic cloves

1 cup (250 mL) Italian-style bread crumbs

2 lemons, zested and juiced

½ stick unsalted butter, melted, divided

2 Tbsp (30 mL) Dijon mustard

1 lb (450 g) bunch of asparagus, woody ends snapped off

THIS IS A classic firehouse or family-style weekend meal. Roasting an entire rack of pork with bones in offers tender, juicy and super-flavourful meat. The simple lemon breading really brightens this roast's flavour.

Preheat the oven to 450°F (230°C). Place the rack in a roasting pan, fat side up. Rub the top with olive oil and sprinkle with the salt and pepper. Roast the pork for 30 minutes.

Meanwhile, place the parsley and garlic in the bowl of a food processor and process until they're both finely minced. Add the bread crumbs, lemon zest and 1 Tbsp (15 mL) melted butter and process for a second until combined.

Take the pork out of the oven, brush with the Dijon mustard and then press the parsley–bread crumb mixture on top of the meat. Drizzle with the melted butter and return immediately to the oven and roast for another 30 minutes or until an internal temperature of 155°F (68°C) is reached.

Take the pork out of the oven, remove from the pan to a cutting board and cover with aluminum foil. Allow it to rest for 15 minutes, then cut into chops. Place the asparagus in the roasting pan that the pork was in, toss with the juices and roast the asparagus for about 5 minutes. Remove the asparagus from the oven, season with salt and pepper and drizzle with fresh lemon juice. To serve, plate the asparagus then lay your pork on top.

 SERVES 6

GRILLED HALIBUT
WITH CLEMENTINE QUINOA

QUINOA HAS BECOME quite a popular ingredient to store in our pantry at the firehouse. Having it on hand means a nutritious side dish or salad is always possible. In this recipe it is loaded up with different textures and tastes and serves as a base for a beautiful piece of grilled halibut. I love the firmness of halibut and its mild flavour, which top this salad perfectly.

Peel 2 clementines, reserving the peel and segments separately. Place the clementine peels, ginger and olive oil in a small saucepan over medium heat. As soon as the oil starts to bubble remove from heat, about 2 minutes. Set the oil aside and allow it to steep for 15 minutes while you prepare the rest of the dish. Once steeped, strain and reserve the oil.

Put the quinoa in a small saucepan with the vegetable stock and ½ tsp (2 mL) salt. Bring to a boil over high heat, then reduce heat to maintain a gentle simmer. Cook uncovered for 15 minutes then set aside for another 5 minutes. Transfer the quinoa to a large bowl and fluff with a fork.

Juice the third clementine over a medium bowl, there should be around 2 Tbsp (30 mL) fresh juice. Whisk the clementine juice with the vinegar and honey in a medium bowl. Gradually whisk in 3 Tbsp (45 mL) reserved clementine oil then season with salt and pepper to taste.

Toss quinoa with the dressing, jalapeño, green onions, shallot, black beans and cilantro. Toss the pine nuts into a small dry skillet over medium-low heat. Once they become fragrant, watch them carefully for about 5 minutes, turning frequently so they don't burn. Once toasted, toss them in the salad as well. Slice the reserved clementine segments in half and add them to the salad. Adjust seasoning with salt and pepper to taste.

For the halibut, preheat a grill or grill pan to high heat. Thread the halibut cubes onto the metal skewers. Season the skewers liberally with salt and pepper and brush with the remaining clementine oil. Grill the halibut, basting as you go with the clementine oil, for about 3 minutes per side. Skewers should be nicely charred but still moist on the inside. Remove halibut chunks from the skewers and place 3 pieces on top of each quinoa salad.

SERVES 4–6

3 clementine oranges

8 thin slices fresh ginger

¼ cup (60 mL) extra virgin olive oil

¾ cup (190 mL) quinoa

1½ cups (375 mL) vegetable stock

½ tsp (2 mL) kosher salt + more, to taste

1 Tbsp (15 mL) white wine vinegar

2 tsp (10 mL) honey

1 small jalapeño, minced (with seeds for maximum heat if preferred)

2 green onions (both white and green parts), minced

1 shallot, minced

½ cup (125 mL) black beans, rinsed

2 Tbsp (30 mL) chopped fresh cilantro

¼ cup (60 mL) pine nuts

Freshly ground pepper, to taste

1½ lb (700 g) centre-cut halibut fillet, cut into 2-inch (5 cm) cubes

MEDALLION OF PORK CHARCUTIERE

REGIS CHEVALIER, FORT MCMURRAY FIRE
DEPARTMENT, ALBERTA

1¼ cups (310 mL) butter,
softened, divided

2 lb (900 g) pork tenderloin,
cut into 8 medallions

1 large white onion, diced

½ cup (125 mL) julienned
unsweetened and unflavoured
gherkins

⅓ cup (80 mL) dry white wine

1 cup (250 mL) Dijon mustard

¼ cup (60 mL) flour

¾ cup (190 mL) whipping
cream + 1 Tbsp (15 mL) for
potatoes (optional)

Kosher salt, to taste

Freshly ground pepper, to taste

3 large russet potatoes

1 Tbsp (15 mL) grated garlic

KEEPING THE PROUD firefighters of Fort McMurray well fed and happy is something member Regis Chevalier does with expertise, which shines through in this amazing recipe. The dividends are evident as the Fort McMurray Fire Fighters Association was awarded with the Queen Elizabeth II Diamond Jubilee Medal. These medals honour professional full-time firefighters who have gone above and beyond their duties of protecting the lives and properties of Canadians to perform countless hours of off-duty work on behalf of their fellow firefighters and their local communities. On top of all this, the Fort McMurray Fire Department is also home to one of Canada's top Firefit Combat Challenge Teams. Coined the "toughest two minutes in sport," FireFit is an obstacle course that requires firefighters to use the skills they use in everyday situations—running up stairs, hoisting hose, using forcible entry and dragging a dummy—all in full firefighter gear in a race against the clock. It is an exhausting test of all our physical skills and motivation. Luckily Regis keeps his 130-plus brothers and sisters in Fort McMurray well fueled.

Place a ½ cup (125 mL) of the butter in a large pan over medium heat. Once the butter is melted and bubbling place the medallions in the pan and cook three-quarters of the way through, about 3 minutes per side. Remove the medallions and set aside.

Place the onion in the pan and cook until light brown and soft, about 7 minutes. Once the onion is cooked add the gherkins to the pan and mix well. Deglaze the pan with white wine and simmer away to reduce by three-quarters, or flambé the pan for a show! Add the Dijon mustard and mix well. Reduce the heat to a gentle simmer.

Add flour to ¼ cup (60 mL) butter in a small bowl. Using a fork, mix together until a paste forms and the flour is totally incorporated into the butter. Pour the whipping cream into the pan and simmer, making sure the heat is low enough so that the cream does not boil. Stir in the butter-flour mixture a tablespoon at a time to thicken the sauce. You might not need to use all of it; the thickness of the sauce needs to be creamy but not too thick.

Return the meat to the sauce with any juices and finish cooking over low heat making sure the meat is covered. Season the sauce to taste with salt and pepper and maintain a low heat to keep warm.

Peel and cook the potatoes in a large pot of boiling salted water until soft. Drain the potatoes, add the rest of the butter and garlic and make a mash, seasoning with salt and pepper. Add a touch of cream to loosen potatoes if necessary. To serve smear the mash on a dinner plate, place a couple of medallions on top and spoon the sauce over.

SERVES 4

YIN-YANG SALMON WITH SAUTÉED PORTOBELLO MUSHROOM, SCENTED JASMINE RICE, EDAMAME AND SOY GINGER BEURRE BLANC SAUCE

PETER BURNS, SURREY FIRE DEPARTMENT, BRITISH COLUMBIA

SCENTED JASMINE RICE

1½ cups (375 mL) water

1 cup (250 mL) jasmine rice, rinsed

1 bay leaf

2 whole cloves

PORTOBELLO MUSHROOMS

¼ cup (60 mL) olive oil

2 cloves minced garlic

1 Tbsp (15 mL) minced ginger

¼ cup (60 mL) rice wine vinegar

¼ cup (60 mL) soy sauce

2 Tbsp (30 mL) orange blossom honey

4 portobello mushrooms, wiped clean and stems removed

EDAMAME

2 cups (500 mL) shelled fresh or frozen edamame beans

1 clove minced garlic

1 Tbsp (15 mL) butter

White pepper, to taste

YIN-YANG SALMON

⅓ cup (80 mL) soy sauce

1 Tbsp (15 mL) minced ginger

2 Tbsp (30 mL) olive oil

THE SURREY FIRE service (SFS) protects one of Canada's most innovative and fastest growing communities. The Surrey Fire Fighters Association has had a proud tradition of serving their community since 1957. With the support of the city of Surrey and the SFS, the Firefighters Association administers the Surrey Fire Fighters' Charitable Society, working to fulfill needs that are not met in their community, with special focus on Surrey's children, youth and families. The society has been changing lives in Surrey since it was founded in 1994. Surrey's firefighters have proudly raised millions of dollars for over 50 community-based organizations, with all funds going directly to helping its citizens. Their amazing work has not gone unnoticed, and the Surrey Firefighters Association was awarded Leader of the Decade by their community for the integral part they have played in shaping the culture of Surrey.

Peter Burns is a proud member of this exceptional association and his expertise as a firehouse chef fits right in. The presentation and flavours of his firehouse creation are extraordinary! It is sure to impress even the most discriminating palate and it is truly a work of art.

SCENTED JASMINE RICE In a medium pot bring the water to a boil and add the rice, bay leaf and cloves. Reduce heat to a simmer and cook rice for 5 minutes. Remove from heat and let stand covered for 10 minutes. Remove the bay leaf and cloves before serving.

PORTOBELLO MUSHROOMS Combine all the ingredients and marinate the mushrooms for 20 minutes. Sauté on medium heat until the mushrooms are soft, approximately 10 minutes.

EDAMAME In a pot of boiling water blanch the beans for 1 minute then place in an ice bath to stop the cooking process. In a medium pan, sauté the garlic in the butter on medium heat just until the garlic is soft but does not start to brown. Drain the edamame beans from the ice bath and add to the garlic and butter and heat through. Add pepper to taste.

YIN-YANG SALMON Combine soy sauce, ginger, olive oil, brown sugar and orange juice and marinate salmon for 20 minutes. Preheat the oven to 350°F (175°C).

Remove salmon from the marinade and pat dry with a paper towel. Cut the salmon fillet into 4 equal portions approximately 2 inches (5 cm) wide. Cut each portion in half so that you have 4 pairs of 1-inch (2.5 cm) pieces. Take 1 piece of salmon and dip the cut edge into the black sesame seeds and place it on the cutting board seed-side up. Take the second piece of salmon and dip it into the white sesame seeds and place it seed side up beside the first piece of salmon. Form the 2 pieces of salmon to create the yin-yang design and hold it in place with the strip of aluminum foil. Repeat for the other 3 pairs.

Place the salmon medallions on a lightly oiled baking tray and bake for 12–18 minutes depending on the thickness of the salmon. Remove from the oven and carefully remove the aluminum strip.

ORANGE SOY GINGER BEURRE BLANC SAUCE Combine vinegar, orange juice, wine, orange zest, ginger and the shallot in a small pot and bring to a boil. Reduce the heat and simmer until the mixture is reduced by two-thirds. Using a fine mesh sieve strain into a clean pot. Add the cream and bring to a simmer. Reduce the sauce by half and remove from the heat. Whisk in the butter a little at a time until the sauce is smooth and shiny. Add the chives, salt and pepper.

PORTOBELLO MUSHROOM To plate: using a 3-inch (8 cm) ring mold in the centre of the plate press ⅓ cup (80 mL) cooked rice to form the rice base. Layer the portobello mushroom on the rice and then the salmon on top of the mushroom. Arrange ½ cup (125 mL) edamame beans around the rice and finish off with the beurre blanc sauce around the edamame beans.

SERVES 4

¼ cup (60 mL) brown sugar

⅓ cup (80 mL) fresh orange juice

2–3 lb (900–1400 g) boneless skinless salmon fillet

½ cup (125 mL) white sesame seeds

½ cup (125 mL) black sesame seeds

15-inch (38 cm) long piece of aluminum foil folded down to a 1½-inch (4 cm) wide strip

ORANGE SOY GINGER BEURRE BLANC SAUCE

¼ cup (60 mL) white wine vinegar

¾ cup (190 mL) fresh orange juice

1 cup (250 mL) dry white wine

2 Tbsp (30 mL) orange zest

1 Tbsp (15 mL) minced ginger

¼ cup (60 mL) diced shallot

½ cup (125 mL) heavy cream

1 cup (250 mL) cold unsalted butter, cut into 1-inch (2.5 cm) cubes

Pinch of salt

White pepper, to taste

GARNISH

3 Tbsp (45 mL) diced chives

MUSHROOM, SPINACH AND FETA-STUFFED CHICKEN WITH PARMESAN CREAM SAUCE

JAMES ASKIN, WINDSOR FIRE DEPARTMENT, ONTARIO

3 Tbsp (45 mL) extra virgin olive oil, divided

½ cup (125 mL) chopped onion

1 clove garlic, chopped

1 cup (250 mL) sliced mushrooms

¼ cup (60 mL) white wine

2 cups (500 mL) baby spinach

Kosher salt, to taste

Freshly ground pepper, to taste

½ cup (125 mL) crumbled feta cheese

4 boneless, skinless chicken breasts (about 4 oz/110 g each)

1 tsp (5 mL) paprika, thyme, oregano or garlic (optional)

1 batch Parmesan Cream Sauce (recipe follows)

WHEN AN EMERGENCY situation flares in Canada's southernmost city, Windsor Fire and Rescue Services is always ready and able to assist. Sitting on the Detroit River with the Motor City in direct view, the more than 300 proud members of the Windsor Professional Firefighters Association are deep rooted in their community, and have had a strong presence for a long time. Helping their citizens in need during emergencies is one thing, but Windsor firefighters are also just as well known for their community service. They established the Firefighters' Benefit Fund in 1921. In the early years, its purpose was to help firefighters who had fallen on hard times due to illness, injury or financial difficulties. Fellow firefighters would organize fundraisers and donate what they could to assist their brothers and sisters in times of need. Fast-forward to the present and you will find the Benefit Fund has expanded to helping those less fortunate within their local community. Three of the Benefit Funds' biggest events are the "Buck for Luck," "Chilifest" and "Sparky's Toy Drive." The WPFA appreciates their community's support and will always do what they can, no matter what the request is, in order to make a difference for those in need. Firefighter James Askin is making his mark and contributing to his team in the kitchen as well. His stuffed chicken firehouse specialty turns a regular chicken breast into a superb main that is sure to impress.

Preheat your oven to 350°F (175°C).

Heat olive oil in a pan. Add onion and garlic and cook over moderate heat until clear, about 5 minutes.

Add mushrooms and continue to cook until softened. Add white wine and spinach. Cook until spinach is wilted. Season to taste with salt and pepper and remove from heat; allow cooling for about 5 minutes. Add feta cheese.

Flatten chicken breasts with a mallet between sheets of plastic film. Season the chicken breasts with salt and pepper.

Add 2 Tbsp (30 mL) of the mushroom, spinach and feta mixture to the centre of the chicken breast and roll into a ball with the seam side facing down.

Place on a parchment-lined baking tray and brush with olive oil. You may add seasoning to the olive oil of your choice (paprika, thyme, oregano, garlic).

Bake at 350°F (175°C) for 25 minutes or until an internal temperature of 170°F (77°C) has been reached. Spoon the Parmesan Cream Sauce over top.

PARMESAN CREAM SAUCE For the Parmesan Cream Sauce, melt butter in a small saucepan over medium heat. Add garlic and flour and stir until combined. Slowly whisk in the cream and continue to mix until combined and thickened.

Add Parmesan cheese and season to taste with salt and pepper. Continue to cook until the sauce no longer tastes like flour. Add the parsley just before serving.

SERVES 4

PARMESAN CREAM SAUCE

3 Tbsp (45 mL) butter

1 clove garlic, chopped

3 Tbsp (45 mL) flour

1 cup (250 mL) 18% cream

½ cup (125 mL) Parmesan cheese

¼ cup (60 mL) chopped fresh flat-leaf parsley

Kosher salt, to taste

Freshly ground pepper, to taste

PEI LOBSTER-TOPPED BAKED POTATOES

ALAN TILLEY AND THE CHARLOTTETOWN FIRE DEPARTMENT,
PRINCE EDWARD ISLAND

4 PEI russet potatoes,
scrubbed and dried

2–3 Tbsp (30–45 mL) butter

PEI LOBSTER TOPPING

1 cup (250 mL) fresh PEI lobster
meat, tail and claw, juice
reserved

1 Tbsp (15 mL) lobster juice
(from the meat)

4 oz (110 g) cream cheese

½ cup (125 mL) Miracle Whip

¼ cup (60 mL) sour cream

1 tsp (5 mL) minced fresh
chives

Kosher salt, to taste

Freshly ground pepper,
to taste

ON BEAUTIFUL LITTLE Prince Edward Island, the birthplace of Canadian Confederation, the Charlottetown Fire Department stands watch, ever ready when duty calls. They are a very proud composite fire department consisting of highly dedicated career and volunteer fire personnel, with an active Fire Prevention Division. They are committed to excellence, to mitigating emergencies when they occur and to giving back to their community, raising thousands and thousands of dollars for community-based charities as well as Muscular Dystrophy Canada. Career firefighter Alan Tilley offers his locally inspired firehouse specialty that is soon to be famous, much like the two famous PEI ingredients he utilizes: PEI lobster and russet potatoes!

Preheat the oven to 400°F (200°C).

Place the potatoes directly on the rack in the centre of the oven and bake for 30 minutes. Pierce each potato in a couple spots with a fork and continue to bake until tender, about 30 minutes.

PEI LOBSTER TOPPING While the potatoes are baking prepare the lobster topping by mixing all the ingredients together. Set aside.

ASSEMBLY When the potatoes are done cooking hold each with an oven mitt or towel, remove the top portion of the skin and carefully scoop out most of the potato into a bowl. Mash the potato lightly with fork along with 2–3 Tbsp (30–45 mL) butter and season with salt and pepper. Refill the shells with the potato mixture then spoon the PEI Lobster Topping over the hot baked potatoes.

 SERVES 4

SWORDFISH NIÇOISE

I HAVE MADE this recipe time and time again in my cooking classes and it is always a hit. Any firm-body fish will do for this recipe, but I really love the dense and mild flavour of swordfish, which should be available at any good fishmonger. The niçoise salsa adds brightness and a briny kick that compliments the fish perfectly.

Drizzle the swordfish steaks with 2 Tbsp (305 mL) olive oil and sprinkle with the thyme and rosemary. Marinate at room temperature for about 1 hour.

Heat the remaining olive oil in a frying pan over medium-high heat. Soften the shallot with the garlic for about 3 minutes. Add the olives, anchovies, capers and tomatoes. Deglaze the pan with the wine and bring to a boil. Turn the heat down to low and gently simmer for 10 minutes or until the sauce has thickened, then season sauce to taste with salt and pepper.

Preheat the broiler. Season the swordfish liberally on both sides with salt and pepper and place steaks under the broiler. Cook until medium rare, about 4–6 minutes on each side. Place on individual plates and spoon the sauce on top. Serve immediately and enjoy!

SERVES 6

6 swordfish steaks (about 6 oz/170 g each)

¼ cup (60 mL) olive oil, divided

1 Tbsp (15 mL) fresh thyme

1 Tbsp (15 mL) fresh rosemary, minced

1 shallot, chopped

3 garlic cloves, minced

½ cup (125 mL) chopped sun-cured black olives, pitted

4 anchovy fillets, chopped

3 Tbsp (45 mL) capers, chopped

3 tomatoes, peeled and chopped

½ cup (125 mL) dry white wine

Kosher salt, to taste

Freshly ground pepper, to taste

OVEN-ROASTED LAMB CHOPS WITH MINT CHIMICHURRI

CHIMICHURRI IS ONE of those sauces that got so popular in my firehouse I had to create recipes just to use it. At one point I had so many requests for it I was jarring and sending chimichurri throughout the department, even to the chief! This special edition gets mint added in as mint and lamb have a nice little relationship together. We have really great lamb producers in Ontario, and these seared-then-roasted chops can be an excellent hors d'oeuvre or an elegant main.

In a blender purée the mint, parsley, cilantro, jalapeño, shallot, garlic, vinegar, lemon juice and ½ cup (125 mL) oil. Season the chimichurri liberally to taste with salt and pepper.

Preheat the oven to 450°F (230°C). In an ovenproof skillet heat 2 Tbsp (30 mL) of the oil until shimmering. Season the lamb very well with salt and pepper and add each rack to the skillet fat-side down. Brown the racks over high heat, about 4 minutes, turning just once and cooking 4 minutes longer. Transfer the skillet to the oven and roast for about 12 minutes, until medium rare. Transfer the lamb to a carving board and let rest for 10 minutes.

Carve the racks into chops and serve with a dollop of mint chimichurri on top.

SERVES 4

1 cup (250 mL) fresh mint

1 cup (250 mL) fresh flat-leaf parsley

½ cup (125 mL) fresh cilantro

1 small jalapeño, seeded and coarsely chopped

1 small shallot, coarsely chopped

3 garlic cloves, coarsely chopped

2 Tbsp (30 mL) red wine vinegar

2 Tbsp (30 mL) lemon juice

½ cup (125 mL) + 2 Tbsp (30 mL) extra virgin olive oil, divided

Kosher salt, to taste

Freshly ground pepper, to taste

2 six-rib racks of lamb (about 1½ lb/700 g each)

THAI RED CURRY MUSSELS

1 Tbsp (15 mL) peanut oil

1 stalk lemongrass, white part only, crushed and minced

1 tsp (5 mL) minced ginger

1 tsp (5 mL) minced garlic

2 Tbsp (30 mL) Thai red curry paste

½ cup (125 mL) white wine

1⅔ cups (410 mL) coconut milk

2 Tbsp (30 mL) fish sauce

2 Tbsp (30 mL) fresh lime juice

2½ lb (1.2 kg) mussels, scrubbed and debearded

2 Tbsp (30 mL) chopped fresh cilantro

5–6 green onions, sliced on a bias

Baguette, torn into pieces for dipping

THIS IS MY wife Andrea and my go-to date-night meal. It is a highly flavourful dish that brings back sweet memories of beautiful Thailand. This recipe also doubles as a pretty great firehouse meal as it is very simple and quite inexpensive to make, and that is firehouse meal criteria. Make sure you have lots of fresh baguette to soak up all the wonderful Thai curry sauce.

Heat the peanut oil in a Dutch oven over medium heat until shimmering. Add the lemongrass, ginger, garlic and curry paste to the pot. Sauté for a few minutes and stir often just until everything becomes fragrant. Deglaze the pot with the wine then add in the coconut milk, fish sauce and lime juice and bring to a simmer, stirring occasionally to allow the flavours to come together.

Add the mussels to the pot and stir in well to make sure they are coated with everything. Cover the pot and let steam until open, about 5 minutes. During the last minute of cooking, add the cilantro and green onion. Ladle the mussels into soup bowls and cover with the cooking liquid. Serve with baguette to soak up all the amazing sauce.

SERVES 2 WITH LEFTOVERS

THE INVERTED
SURF AND TURF

TURN THE OLD classic upside down! A very beautiful and elegant main course of seared rare tuna steak (my favourite) topped with beef tartar (a close second).

SURF To make the surf marinade, whisk all the ingredients apart from the tuna in a bowl to emulsify. Pour over the tuna, coating on both sides, and allow to marinate for 30 minutes. While the tuna marinates prepare the turf.

Heat a grill or grill pan over medium-high heat. Remove the tuna from the marinade and pat dry with paper towel. Season the tuna on all sides with a fair amount of salt and pepper and reserve the marinade. Lay the tuna in the hot pan and sear for approximately 1–2 minutes on each side ensuring the inside is still rare. Remove tuna to a cutting board and drizzle marinade over as it rests.

TURF Toss the greens with a drizzle of olive oil, a squeeze of lemon juice and season with the smoked sea salt flakes and pepper. Plate the greens and slice the tuna into ¼-inch (6 mm) thick slices and place on top. Using a small ring mold form the beef tartar on top of the tuna and serve with a couple of the toast points on the side.

SERVES 6

SURF

2 garlic cloves, minced

1 tsp (5 mL) Dijon mustard

3 Tbsp (45 mL) champagne vinegar

½ lemon, juiced

2 Tbsp (30 mL) chopped fresh flat-leaf parsley

2 Tbsp (30 mL) minced fresh tarragon

Kosher salt, to taste

Freshly ground pepper, to taste

½ cup (125 mL) extra virgin olive oil

2 lb (900 g) ahi tuna steak

TURF

1½ cups (375 mL) mixed baby greens

1 Tbsp (15 mL) extra virgin olive oil

1 lemon, juiced

Smoked sea salt flakes, to taste

Freshly ground pepper, to taste

1 batch Beef Tartar (see page 11)

12 slices of artisan white bread, toasted, buttered and quartered

WEST COAST SOCKEYE SALMON WITH ARUGULA PESTO, SUCCOTASH SALAD AND GOAT CHEESE SMASHED POTATOES

ADAM SEAWARD AND THE MAPLE RIDGE FIRE DEPARTMENT, BRITISH COLUMBIA

1 Tbsp (15 mL) olive oil

6 salmon fillets (about 4–6 oz/110–170 g each)

Kosher salt, to taste

Freshly ground pepper, to taste

1 batch Arugula Pesto (recipe follows)

SUCCOTASH SALAD

½ red onion, diced into ¼-inch (6 mm) pieces

1 red bell pepper, cut into ½-inch (1 cm) pieces

2 carrots, shredded

¾ cup (190 mL) fresh corn

½ cup (125 mL) edamame beans

1½ cups (375 mL) fresh flat-leaf parsley

2 tsp (10 mL) fresh thyme

¼ cup (60 mL) extra virgin olive oil

2 Tbsp (30 mL) balsamic vinegar

1 cup (250 mL) pea or radish shoots

Kosher salt, to taste

Freshly ground pepper, to taste

IN THIS BEAUTIFUL region of British Columbia, flanked by two mountain ranges and the Fraser River, the professional firefighters of Maple Ridge are a highly trained team ready to provide many services to their community. From the traditional role of fire suppression they also work diligently to hone their skills in all aspects of medical response and multiple types of rescue. They are also proud of the many volunteer hours spent raising awareness and funds for various charitable organizations in their community and province. From car washes supporting the British Columbia Burn Fund, to boot drives and sponsoring local events, Maple Ridge firefighters are pillars in their community and are always willing to lend their support. They also support their hometown by priding themselves on eating fresh and local.

When I reached out to Adam Seaward and the Maple Ridge firefighters for a locally inspired recipe, his association enthusiastically jumped at the chance to highlight their beautiful community. Firefighters in Maple Ridge often gather together at one of their favourite local establishments, the Big Feast Bistro. While pondering which of their firehouse recipes to share they thought they would reach out to their favourite source, chef and owner Mike Mulcahy, for a little inspiration that would really make their community proud. If Mike and his Big Feast Bistro sound familiar that's because he appeared on the Food Network's *You Gotta Eat Here,* and for very good reason! Mike shares the same philosophy and pride in his community as his local firefighters and he assisted them in creating this beautiful dish. It truly represents the bounty of their land—wild sockeye salmon and fresh local produce—to form an inspired main course. You gotta eat this!

Preheat your oven to 350°F (175°C).

Heat the olive oil in a pan on medium heat. Season the salmon fillet on both sides with salt and pepper and place into the oiled pan. Cook salmon for 5 minutes flipping once. Finish cooking the salmon until cooked through, approximately 5–10 minutes more in the oven.

SUCCOTASH SALAD To make the salad, toss all ingredients except the shoots, salt and pepper and fold until well coated. Toss in the shoots, season with salt and pepper and serve.

GOAT CHEESE SMASHED POTATOES To make the smashed potatoes, cut potatoes in half and rinse under cold water to rinse away excess starch. Place potatoes in pot and top with cold salted water. Bring the potatoes to a rolling boil, strain and mash with potato masher until no large lumps remain. Add the milk and butter and continue to mash. Add the parsley, cheese and garlic, season with salt and pepper and mix until incorporated.

To serve, make a bed of the smashed potatoes and lay a salmon fillet on top. Spoon the arugula pesto over top of the salmon and serve the succotash salad alongside.

ARUGULA PESTO In a blender or food processor, blend the shoots, arugula, spinach, Parmesan, hazelnuts, parsley and roasted garlic together to form a thick paste. Slowly add the oil, lemon juice and vinegar and process until pesto is smooth with no lumps. Season the pesto to taste with salt and pepper.

SERVES 6

GOAT CHEESE SMASHED POTATOES

2½ lb (1.2 kg) baby potatoes, skin on

1 cup (250 mL) milk

¼ cup (60 mL) butter

1 Tbsp (15 mL) fresh flat-leaf parsley

¼ cup (60 mL) goat cheese

6 cloves roasted garlic

Kosher salt, to taste

Freshly ground pepper, to taste

ARUGULA PESTO

1 cup (250 mL) sunflower shoots

2 cups (500 mL) arugula

2 cups (500 mL) spinach

½ cup (125 mL) Parmesan cheese

½ cup (125 mL) hazelnuts

2 cups (500 mL) fresh flat-leaf parsley

6 cloves roasted garlic

1 cup (250 mL) extra virgin olive oil

2 Tbsp (30 mL) lemon juice

2 Tbsp (30 mL) apple cider vinegar

Kosher salt, to taste

Freshly ground pepper, to taste

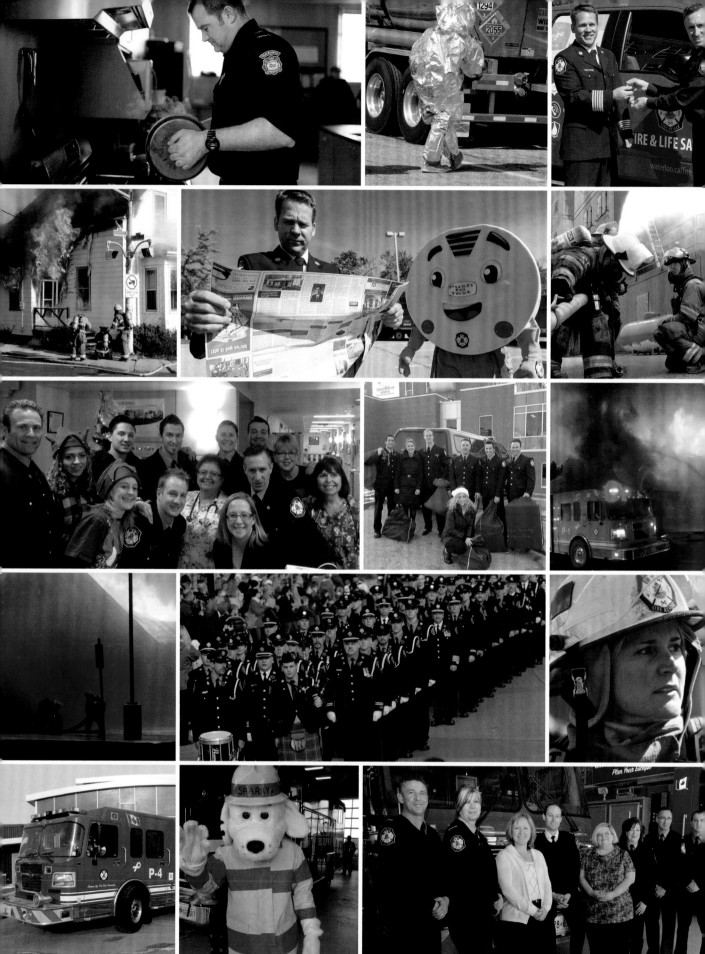

4TH ALARM
THE SWEET FINISH

CLASSIC CRÈME CARAMEL

2 cups (500 mL) heavy cream

1 cup (250 mL) milk

½ vanilla bean, split and seeds scraped out

1 cup (250 mL) sugar, divided

3 egg yolks

2 eggs

Pinch of kosher salt

½ cup (125 mL) sugar

DO NOT BE intimidated by this elegant-yet-simple dessert. Once you have perfected the easy process of making the custard and caramel, this dessert comes together in no time and it can even be made a day or so in advance.

Preheat the oven to 325°F (160°C). Heat the cream and milk in a medium saucepan over medium heat until it just barely begins to simmer. Split the vanilla bean in half and scrape the seeds into the cream; reserve the vanilla pod for another use. Meanwhile, in a medium bowl slowly whisk ½ cup (125 mL) sugar into the egg yolks and eggs until pale and fluffy. Slowly whisk the hot cream and milk into the sugar-yolk mixture. Strain the mixture through a fine sieve into a clean bowl. Add salt.

Arrange 6 ramekins in a baking dish with deep sides and set aside. Put remaining ½ cup (125 mL) sugar in a clean saucepan. Carefully add just enough water to just cover and dissolve the sugar. Set the pot over high heat.

After a few minutes, the mixture will come to a boil; a few minutes more and the water will evaporate and start to colour. Swirl the pan around gently to even out the caramelization. Once the sugar has started to caramelize watch it carefully. It takes just seconds for caramel to go from great to burnt.

When the caramel is an even, rich brown, remove it from the heat and carefully pour it into the ramekins. Caramel at this stage is over 300°F (150°C), so be extremely careful when handling it. Divide it evenly so that each ramekin is covered with a thin layer of dark brown caramel.

Pour the custard into the caramel-lined ramekins. Carefully fill the baking dish with hot water to come halfway up the sides of the ramekins. Cover the dish with foil and bake until just set, about 35–40 minutes. Start checking early, as baking time will depend on the thickness and depth of your ramekins and baking dish. Carefully remove the baking dish from the oven and let the ramekins cool in the water bath. Refrigerate at least 2 hours to fully set or up to 2 days.

To serve, place ramekins in hot water for about 15 seconds. Run a thin knife around the edge of the custard and invert onto a dessert plate, gently tapping to release the custard. Allow any caramel to drizzle on top.

SERVES 6–8

CHOCOLATE PB AND J BARS

Trays of desserts are a big hit in the firehouse. Often someone from the team is bringing in a tray of goodies from home, or someone from the community is dropping off their baked specialty for us, and you better be quick to grab one as sweets tend to disappear in a flash! Everyone in my firehouse loves the taste of classic peanut butter and jelly so this firehouse favourite was a thoughtful creation to transform the beloved sandwich with the addition of chocolate (why not?) into a portable cookie bar.

Preheat oven to 350°F (175°C). Grease an 8 × 8–inch (20 × 20 cm) baking dish and line with parchment paper, leaving enough overhang to grip and remove the bars after they've cooled. Set aside.

In a large mixing bowl whisk together the flour, baking powder and salt.

In another bowl use electric beaters to combine the peanut butter, butter and brown sugar and beat until creamy, about 3–4 minutes. Add the egg and beat until well incorporated. Mix in the vanilla extract. With the beaters on low, gradually add the flour mixture a little at a time. Mix until mostly incorporated, a few streaks are okay, then fold in the chocolate chips.

Press three-quarters of the cookie dough in the bottom of the prepared pan. Layer the cherry jam on top of that.

Grab handfuls of the remaining cookie dough and break it up over the top of the jam so you have crumbles everywhere. Bake the bars for about 30 minutes or until the top is golden in colour.

Cool completely, then grab the edges of the parchment paper and lift straight up to remove from the pan. Cut, serve and enjoy. Everyone loves the taste of classic peanut butter and jelly and now you can take it anywhere!

MAKES 9 BARS

1½ cups (375 mL) all-purpose flour

½ tsp (2 mL) baking powder

¼ tsp (1 mL) kosher salt

1 cup (250 mL) natural crunchy peanut butter

¼ cup (60 mL) unsalted butter, softened

¾ cup (190 mL) lightly packed light brown sugar

1 large egg

1 tsp (5 mL) pure vanilla extract

1½ cups (375 mL) mixture of chocolate chips (dark, semi-sweet and Skor)

2 cups (500 mL) cherry jam

KEY LIME PIE IN A JAR WITH COINTREAU STRAWBERRIES

4 large eggs

4 large egg yolks, reserving the whites

1 cup + 1 Tbsp (265 mL) sugar, divided

½ tsp (2 mL) salt

¾ cup (190 mL) freshly squeezed key lime juice

¾ cup (190 mL) heavy cream

1 tsp (5 mL) pure vanilla extract

¾ cup (190 mL) graham cracker crumbs

3 Tbsp (45 mL) unsalted butter, melted

COINTREAU STRAWBERRIES

1 lb (450 g) fresh strawberries, thinly sliced

¼ cup (60 mL) sugar

1–2 Tbsp (15–30 mL) Cointreau or orange-flavoured liqueur

THESE PORTABLE LITTLE desserts offer all the bright tart flavours of a really good Key Lime Pie, my favourite dessert, but in a light and airy mousse. The Cointreau-infused strawberries add great colour and well . . . Cointreau!

In a saucepan whisk together the eggs, yolks, ¾ cup (190 mL) sugar, salt and lime juice. Cook over medium-low heat while stirring constantly until it thickens, about 10 minutes. The key lime curd is done when it is as thick as pudding and coats the back of a spoon or spatula. Press through a fine mesh strainer and cool.

Whip the egg whites and remaining ¼ cup (60 mL) sugar until they reach stiff peaks. Add a third of the whites to the chilled key lime curd and mix to lighten the texture of the curd. Gently fold the remaining whites in.

Whip the heavy cream with the vanilla extract until stiff peaks form. Fold the whipped cream gently into the key lime mousse. Fold just until the cream is smoothly incorporated and refrigerate until ready to eat.

Combine the graham cracker crumbs, 1 Tbsp (15 mL) sugar and melted butter and set aside.

COINTREAU STRAWBERRIES Mix the strawberries, sugar and liqueur in a bowl and let the berries sit for at least 30 minutes, so they release some of their juices.

ASSEMBLY To serve fill the bottom of a mason jar with the key lime mousse, top with the strawberries and then sprinkle the graham cracker crumbs on top.

MAKES 6 JARS

FRESH PEACH AND MASCARPONE SORBET

FIREFIGHTERS REALLY ARE connoisseurs of frozen dessert. If it's your birthday or you happen to be working an extra shift, then it is expected that you reward your brothers and sisters with a little frozen treat! I thought I had better learn to make a no-fuss homemade version, highlighting fresh fruit in its peak season. No special equipment necessary and you can use any seasonal fruit you wish for this sorbet.

Place the water, ½ cup (125 mL) sugar and mint in a small pan and bring to a simmer, stirring occasionally to help dissolve the sugar. Let simmer over low heat to steep the mint for about 5 minutes. Strain the mint from the simple syrup and discard.

In a food processor combine chopped peaches with the remaining sugar. Run the machine to purée the peaches. Add the mascarpone cheese, lemon juice and salt. Run the machine until the mascarpone cheese is fully incorporated. Add the mint simple syrup and run the machine to combine well. Place the mixture in a glass dish and place the dish in the freezer. The mixture will take about 4 hours to freeze.

To serve, spoon the mixture into chilled bowls and top with the finely sliced peaches and fresh mint.

SERVES 6

1 cup (250 mL) water

½ cup (125 mL) + 1 Tbsp (15 mL) sugar

½ cup (125 mL) chopped fresh mint leaves + more for serving

2 cups (500 mL) chopped peaches (frozen is okay too) + 1 cup (250 mL) finely sliced for serving

½ cup (125 mL) mascarpone cheese

3 Tbsp (45 mL) lemon juice

Pinch of salt

CHOCOLATE RASPBERRY SOUP

1½ cups (375 mL)
heavy cream

1 Tbsp (15 mL) butter

2 Tbsp (30 mL) sugar

½ lb (225 g) bittersweet
chocolate, chopped

¼ cup (60 mL) raspberry purée

1 cup (250 mL) fresh
raspberries

2 Tbsp (30 mL) roughly
chopped hazelnuts

1 Tbsp (15 mL) fresh mint,
thinly sliced

Pinch of salt

2 Tbsp (30 mL) raspberry
liqueur

½ cup (125 mL) sweetened
whipped cream, for garnish

Small piece bittersweet
chocolate to shave,
for garnish

THIS CHILLED SOUP is summer dessert at its finest, especially during fresh raspberry season. Its unique flavour and bright vibrant colour will make you wonder why you have never had dessert soup before.

In a small saucepan bring the cream, butter and sugar to just a boil. Remove from the heat and stir in the chopped chocolate so that it melts completely. Stir in the raspberry purée.

In another bowl gently fold together the raspberries, hazelnuts, mint, salt and the raspberry liqueur.

In a shallow soup bowl pour in the chocolate soup. Place a nice spoonful of the raspberry-hazelnut salad in the centre and garnish with a small spoonful of whipped cream and shaved bittersweet chocolate.

SERVES 4–6

CHRISTMAS RUMNOG CRÈME BRÛLÉE

1 extra-large egg

4 extra-large egg yolks

½ cup (125 mL) sugar

1 cup (250 mL) heavy cream

2 cups (500 mL) eggnog

1 tsp (5 mL) pure vanilla

Dash of cinnamon

Dash of nutmeg

¼ cup (60 mL) dark rum

¼ cup (60 mL) crushed candy canes

MY WIFE AND I just love Christmas and celebrating the holiday season. It is our favourite time of year! Having missed Christmas in the past due to working at the firehouse we have learned to celebrate as often and whenever we can during the holiday season by having gatherings of family and friends with lots of food and drink. This colourful and unique brûlée is a great twist on the classic and a very festive way to finish off any holiday meal.

Preheat the oven to 300°F (150°C).

In a large bowl whisk the egg, egg yolks and sugar together until pale and smooth.

Heat the cream and eggnog in a small saucepan until it just starts to simmer. Remove from the heat and slowly and add the cream mixture to the eggs, a little at a time, whisking constantly. Add the vanilla, cinnamon, nutmeg and rum. For a super-smooth custard strain this mixture through a fine mesh sieve into a clean bowl to remove any little egg bits.

Pour the custard into six 8-oz (225 g) ramekins until three-quarters full.

Place the ramekins in a baking pan and carefully pour hot water into the pan to come halfway up the sides of the ramekins. Cover with foil and bake for 35–40 minutes, until the custards are set when gently shaken. Remove the custards from the water bath, cool to room temperature and refrigerate until firm.

To serve, spread 1 Tbsp (15 mL) crushed candy can evenly on the top of each ramekin and heat with a kitchen blowtorch, or under a broiler for a few minutes until the candy cane melts and caramelizes. Allow to sit at room temperature for a minute until the caramelized sugar hardens.

SERVES 6–8

GRILLED CHOCOLATE SANDWICHES

I HAVE LEARNED from cooking in the firehouse that as long as you have a loaf of bread and a well-stocked pantry and refrigerator then you only need a little creativity to create something exciting. A stuffed dessert sandwich with melted chocolate is a pretty good example of that!

Lay 6 pound cake slices on a work surface. Spread each of the slices with at least 1 Tbsp (15 mL) peanut butter, cherry jam and a few slices of banana.

Top each slice with 2 chocolate squares. Make a sandwich with the remaining cake slices. Brush melted butter on both sides of each sandwich and sprinkle each side with a little of the brown sugar

Using a non-stick skillet grill the sandwiches over medium-low heat until chocolate has melted and bread is a golden brown. Dust sandwiches with icing sugar and garnish with fresh raspberries. Serve while still warm.

SERVES 6

Twelve ½-inch (1 cm) thick slices pound cake

6 Tbsp (90 mL) peanut butter

6 Tbsp (90 mL) cherry jam

2 bananas, thinly sliced

3½ oz (100 g) pkg good-quality thin chocolate squares (Ghirardelli, for example)

⅓ cup (80 mL) unsalted butter, melted

¼ cup (60 mL) brown sugar, for sprinkling

3 Tbsp (45 mL) icing sugar, for garnish

1 cup (250 mL) fresh raspberries, for garnish

GRILLED PINEAPPLE WITH BOURBON CARAMEL SAUCE

GRILLED FRUIT IS one of my favourite summertime desserts. Adding a little char really brings out the natural sweetness in fruit. Along with pineapple try grilling peaches, bananas or even watermelon. The Bourbon Caramel Sauce is the real hit in this recipe and you will find yourself drizzling it on just about everything!

Cut the body of pineapple into 6 slices of even width. Halve each slice and set in a baking pan.

Pour the glaze over the pineapple to marinade for about 10 minutes.

Preheat your grill to high heat. Remove the pineapple slices from the marinade and place them on the grill. Grill the pineapple, basting as you go with the glaze until you have nice char marks, about 3 minutes per side. Remove pineapple from the grill and drizzle with any remaining glaze. Serve warm with a generous scoop of vanilla bean ice cream.

BOURBON CARAMEL SAUCE Mix all the remaining ingredients except the ice cream together in a saucepan and bring to a boil over medium-high heat. Stir well, reduce the heat to maintain a simmer and continue to cook until the sauce thickens into a glaze, about 5 minutes.

SERVES 6

1 pineapple, top and bottom and skin removed

Vanilla bean ice cream, for serving

1 batch Bourbon Caramel Sauce (recipe follows)

BOURBON CARAMEL SAUCE

½ cup (125 mL) bourbon

½ cup (125 mL) brown sugar

¼ cup (60 mL) grapeseed oil

2 Tbsp (30 mL) butter

1½ Tbsp (23 mL) ground cinnamon

½ tsp (2 mL) kosher salt

¼ tsp (1 mL) ground cloves

Pinch of cayenne

GUINNESS ICE CREAM FLOATS

WHEN I WAS a kid my Dad would always make root beer floats for a little weekend treat. Now, just for my Dad, here is an easy grown-up version that I like to feature in my "Dude Food" cooking classes.

Place ice cream in a tall glass. Pour espresso over top, then add Guinness and then the Irish Cream. Serve with a straw and a long spoon.

SERVES 1

3 scoops butter pecan ice cream

1 Tbsp (15 mL) hot espresso

¼ cup (60 mL) Guinness stout

2 Tbsp (30 mL) Irish cream

MANGO STICKY RICE
WITH COCONUT CREAM

1 cup (250 mL) dry Thai sweet or sticky rice (available in Asian groceries)

1⅔ cups (410 mL) coconut milk

3 Tbsp (45 mL) raw sugar, divided

2 pinches of kosher salt, divided

1⅔ cups (410 mL) coconut cream

2 ripe mangos, peeled and sliced

3 Tbsp (45 mL) toasted sesame seeds, for garnish

3 Tbsp (45 mL) toasted coconut, for garnish

12 sprigs fresh mint, for garnish

THIS DESSERT IS inspired by my Thai honeymoon where we would find this on just about every street corner. It is a great firehouse dessert because, other than the ripe mangoes, everything to make this dessert can be found in your pantry and you can prepare it in a flash! Using ripe mangoes gives this dessert just the right amount of sweetness.

Soak dry sticky rice in water for about 1 hour. Drain the rice and rinse it thoroughly. You may have to repeat this step to make sure most of the starch is rinsed from the rice. Pour about 1 cup (250 mL) water into a saucepan, place the rice in a steamer and insert the steamer inside the saucepan. Cover tightly and steam over low to medium heat for 20 minutes.

You will make 2 coconut sauces to go on the rice; while the rice is steaming, make the first. Pour the coconut milk into a small saucepan and stir in 2 Tbsp (30 mL) sugar and a pinch of salt. Warm over medium heat stirring frequently for 5 minutes. Do not let the sauce boil.

When the rice is done slowly pour the warm coconut milk sauce over the rice and gently fold it in, allowing it to absorb into the rice. You want the milk to coat the rice but not leave puddles, so add the warmed coconut milk carefully—you might not need all of it.

Set the rice aside for about 15 minutes to finish absorbing the coconut milk.

While the rice is standing warm the coconut cream in a saucepan over low heat and stir in 1 Tbsp (15 mL) sugar and a pinch of salt. Simmer over low heat until the cream thickens. Set aside.

To serve, mold about ⅓ cup (80 mL) coconut sticky rice in a ramekin, then unmold on a plate. Arrange mango slices on top and drizzle with the coconut cream sauce. Sprinkle with a few toasted sesame seeds, toasted coconut and garnish with a mint sprig. Enjoy while still warm!

 SERVES 6

MAPLE CINNAMON MONKEY BREAD

THIS MONKEY BREAD is a weekend treat at the firehouse. It presents beautifully once it's set out and gets torn apart in a hurry! It could be dessert or a welcome addition to any brunch menu.

Preheat oven to 350°F (175°C). Grease a large Bundt pan with butter.

Combine the sugar and cinnamon in a large bowl.

Remove the biscuit dough from their canisters and separate into 16 biscuits. Use a sharp knife to cut each biscuit into quarters. Place the pieces in the bowl with the cinnamon and sugar and mix well. Arrange in the Bundt pan in a single layer and sprinkle the layer with chopped pecans.

In a small bowl combine the butter, brown sugar and maple syrup. Spoon the mixture evenly over the biscuit pieces.

Bake 25–30 minutes or until golden brown and cooked through. Allow bread to cool in pan for 10 minutes. Carefully invert onto serving plate and serve warm.

SERVES 6–8

½ cup (125 mL) sugar

1 Tbsp (15 mL) ground cinnamon

Two 16-oz (473 mL) cans store-bought buttermilk biscuit dough (such as Pillsbury), refrigerated

½ cup (125 mL) chopped pecans

¾ cup (190 mL) butter, melted + more for greasing

1 cup (250 mL) firmly packed brown sugar

¼ cup (60 mL) maple syrup

S'MORES SUNDAE

SUNDAES ARE A really simple way to have fun with dessert, and they are a regular treat in the firehouse. This easy and decadent twist on everyone's campfire classic might surpass the original, with a homemade chocolate ganache, toasted marshmallow and lots of ice cream!

Preheat oven to 325°F (160°C) and line a baking tray with parchment paper. Add the graham crackers to a food processor and process into fine crumbs. Add the sugar, butter and salt and pulse until the mixture is well incorporated. Pour out onto baking tray and form into one large "cookie." Bake until light golden brown, about 15 minutes. Let cool completely then break into crumbles.

Preheat oven on broil. Lay marshmallows on a parchment-lined baking tray in a single layer and place under the broiler for just a couple of minutes until browned well all over. Remove and set aside.

Finely chop the chocolate and place in bowl. Heat the heavy cream over medium heat until just starting to simmer. Pour the heavy cream over the chocolate and fold until the chocolate melts and it becomes a smooth ganache.

Place 1 scoop each of vanilla and chocolate ice cream in a parfait glass or bowl. Layer your sundae with dark chocolate ganache, graham cracker crumbles and a toasted marshmallow or two on top.

SERVES 6

12 graham crackers

3 Tbsp (45 mL) brown sugar

1 stick unsalted butter, melted

Pinch of kosher salt

40 large marshmallows

½ lb (225 g) good-quality dark chocolate

½ cup (125 mL) heavy cream

2 cups (500 mL) vanilla bean ice cream

2 cups (500 mL) chocolate chunk ice cream

STRAWBERRY RHUBARB GALETTE

10 × 10 inch (25 × 25 cm) sheet puff pastry

2 cups (500 mL) strawberries, thickly sliced

1 lb (450 g) very red fresh rhubarb stalks, cut crosswise ½ inch (1 cm) thick

¾ cup (190 mL) brown sugar

2 Tbsp (30 mL) all-purpose flour

2 tsp (10 mL) fresh lemon juice

1 tsp (5 mL) pure vanilla extract

1 egg

1 Tbsp (15 mL) whole milk

¼ cup (60 mL) cold unsalted butter, cut into small pieces

1 cup (250 mL) fresh whipped cream, for serving

THIS RUSTIC FRENCH tart is best when fresh strawberries and rhubarb are in their peak season. Store-bought puff pastry makes this fabulous dessert a breeze and will make you look like a star!

Preheat the oven to 400°F (200°C). Line a large rimmed baking tray with parchment paper. On a lightly floured surface roll the puff pastry out to about ⅛ inch (3 mm) thick. Transfer to the baking tray and refrigerate the pastry for 10 minutes.

In a large bowl toss the strawberries with the rhubarb, sugar, flour, lemon juice and vanilla. Spread on the pastry to within 2 inches (5 cm) of the edge. Fold the edge over the filling and pleat it very rustically.

Make an egg wash by beating the egg and milk together. Lightly brush the dough with the egg wash.

Dot the filling with the butter and bake the galette in the centre of the oven for about 35 minutes, or until the fruit is bubbling and the pastry is golden brown. Let the galette cool slightly before cutting into wedges and top with a dollop of fresh whipped cream.

SERVES 6

STOUT CHOCOLATE CAKE

TREVOR MITCHELL, SARNIA FIRE DEPARTMENT, ONTARIO

WHEN YOU BRING a dessert into the firehouse for all of your team to share you instantly become the most popular firefighter in the room! All kidding aside, sometimes it takes just this small gesture to really boost the morale of a crew during a long tour. Firefighter Trevor Mitchell likes to reward his crew at Sarnia Fire Rescue with this delicious and unique stout chocolate cake, featuring stout beer and a little Irish Cream in the cream cheese frosting for something special.

Grease a large cake pan or Bundt pan. Preheat the oven to 325°F (160°C).

In a large bowl, whisk together the flour, cocoa and baking soda. In a seperate bowl, whisk the remaining cake ingredients. Add the wet ingredients to the dry and mix thoroughly so everything is well moistened. Pour into the prepared pan and place into the centre of the oven. Bake for about an hour—when the cake is pricked with a fork it should come out clean. Remove from the pan and set aside to cool.

ICING Mix all of the icing ingredients thoroughly. Once the cake is cooled spread the icing over top. Cake can be chilled until ready to serve.

SERVES 6–8

2 cups (500 mL) flour

½ cup (125 mL) dark cocoa

2 tsp (10 mL) baking soda

1 cup (250 mL) stout beer
(I like Young's Double Chocolate
Stout or Guinness)

2 eggs

½ cup (125 mL) unsalted butter,
melted + more for greasing

¾ cup (190 mL) thick sour
cream

1 tsp (5 mL) vanilla

2 cups (500 mL) sugar

ICING

½ lb (225 g) cream cheese

1¼ cups (310 mL) icing sugar

½ cup (125 mL) Irish cream

THE BEST CHOCOLATE CHIP COOKIES

SCOTT MORRISON, MISSISSAUGA FIRE
DEPARTMENT, ONTARIO

2 cups (500 mL) butter

1 cup (250 mL) brown sugar

½ cup (125 mL) white sugar

2 eggs

2 tsp (10 mL) real vanilla

2 cups (500 mL) all-purpose flour

1 tsp (5 mL) baking soda

1 tsp (5 mL) salt

2 cups (500 mL) chocolate chips (I use Hershey pure chocolate chips)

GROWING UP I always enjoyed these cookies (which are excellent dipped in a cup of milk), whether it was my grandma making them on holidays or my mom on a not-so-regular basis. While attending college away from home I realized I couldn't get enough to satisfy my cravings and decided to learn how to bake them myself. After many failed attempts, I feel I have mastered the recipe. Now I am said to make the best batch of cookies throughout my family.

Coming to the fire department I quickly learned that food is a big part of your day and the preparation of that food with your truck mates is great for team building and station camaraderie. I had to bring my best to the table; I mean everyone has to have a specialty and we seemed to be lacking in the baking department. In stepped my cookies, and lo and behold they were a hit. Since starting on the job in 2004, I have made many cookies, and I hope others will sit down with a cup of milk to enjoy them! (Intro by Scott Morrison.)

Preheat your oven to 375°F (190°C).

Cream together the butter, brown sugar and white sugar. Beat in the eggs and vanilla.

In a separate bowl combine the flour, baking soda and salt. Gradually beat the flour mixture into the liquid mixture. Stir in the chocolate chips.

Drop small spoonfuls of batter onto an ungreased cookie sheet. Bake for 8–12 minutes, until golden brown on top and still nice and soft in the middle. Allow to cool slightly before serving.

MAKES 12 COOKIES

OREO ICE CREAM CAKE

JEFF DERRAUGH AND DIANE MCNAUGHTON, UNITED
FIREFIGHTERS OF WINNIPEG, MANITOBA

8 cups (2 L) of your favourite vanilla ice cream

1 lb (450 g) box of Oreo cookies (more if you're unable to resist the temptation of snacking while you work)

⅓ cup (80 mL) melted butter

1.5 oz (45 g) bag of mini Oreo cookies, for garnish

A LONG-HELD TRADITION on the Winnipeg Fire Department is to bring a cake to work on your birthday. When June 6 rolls around, I always have an Oreo Ice Cream Cake in tow. All you need to know is how quick and easy it is to make! Do you have kids coming over? I've yet to meet a little—or big—nose miner that doesn't love this quick and easy classic. Hey and it's a great dessert for any confirmed chocaholic. Oh well, it appears that the Twelve Step program is out the window . . . again! Thanks to our friend Diane McNaughton for this recipe. (Intro by Jeff Derraugh.)

Allow the ice cream to soften on the counter while you get your butt going on the crust.

Crush up, munch, mangle and totally deface the entire bag of Oreo cookies with a rolling pin, food processor or under the wheels of your SUV, ensuring that the vehicle is in 4-wheel low for this operation. The consistency should be fairly fine.

Place 2 cups (500 mL) crunched up cookies in a bowl, add the melted butter and mix it all together with a spoon.

Press the mixture onto the bottom of a lightly greased springform pan to form the crust. Depending on the size of the pan you're using you may have to make a little more crust. Crush, crush!

Take the remaining crushed Oreos, minus 2 Tbsp (30 mL), and blend them with a wooden spoon into the softened ice cream. Pour the ice cream mixture over the cookie crust. Sprinkle the reserved 2 Tbsp (30 mL) mangled Oreos over the top.

Place mini Oreos over the top, in a circle around the edge or throughout as desired. Hey, presentation is important! Freeze for several hours until the cake is completely frozen and set.

SERVES 6–8

WHISKY PEACH COBBLER

1 cup (250 mL) all-purpose flour

1 tsp (5 mL) baking powder

½ tsp (2 mL) salt

2 large eggs

1½ cups (375 mL) sugar, divided

2 Tbsp (30 mL) soft butter + extra for the pan

¼ cup (60 mL) milk

¼ cup (60 mL) whisky

1 Tbsp (15 mL) lemon juice

1 Tbsp (15 mL) pure vanilla extract

4 large ripe peaches, sliced thin

1 cup (250 mL) heavy cream or 2 cups (500 mL) ice cream, for serving

I REALLY LOVE to stop by roadside fruit and vegetable stands on my way into the firehouse. Not only is it a great way to eat fresh and local but when you buy in season it's also quite inexpensive, not to mention a great way to support your local community. Sometimes when you buy a large basket of peaches you just can't eat them fast enough. Save the super-ripe ones to be the stars and sweetness in this easy and comforting dessert.

Preheat the oven to 375°F (190°C). Butter a square 8- or 9-inch (20 or 23 cm) baking pan.

Whisk together the flour, baking powder and salt in a mixing bowl and set aside. In a separate bowl, whisk together the eggs and 1 cup (250 mL) sugar. To that, add the butter and milk and whisk until mostly even with some small chunks of butter still visible. Add the wet ingredients to the dry ingredients and stir just until everything is moistened. Scrape the batter into the buttered baking pan.

In a saucepan over medium-high heat stir together the remaining ½ cup (125 mL) sugar, whisky, lemon juice and vanilla and bring to a boil. Boil for a few minutes then remove the pan from the heat, add the sliced peaches and toss gently with a spatula to coat the fruit with the caramel syrup. Spoon the fruit and syrup evenly over the cobbler batter in the pan.

Bake the cobbler for 30 minutes, or until the edges are caramelized and the inside is fully set, but still moist. Let cool for 10 minutes before scooping from the pan, or cool for 30 minutes before cutting into 9 squares and serving. Serve with a drizzle of cold heavy cream or ice cream.

SERVES 6–8

WINTER BERRY CRISP

5 cups (1.25 L) frozen mixed berries

¾ cup (190 mL) brown sugar, divided

½ cup + 2 Tbsp (155 mL) all-purpose flour, divided

1 cup (250 mL) large flake oats (not instant)

½ cup (125 mL) packed brown sugar, divided

½ cup (125 mL) chopped pecans or walnuts

½ cup (125 mL) pumpkin seeds

½ tsp (2 mL) cinnamon

Pinch of fresh grated nutmeg

Pinch of kosher salt

1 stick butter, softened + more for greasing

2 cups (500 mL) vanilla bean ice cream, for serving

MAKING ANY TYPE of crisp is really a weekend shift firehouse classic. It is an excellent opportunity to clean out the refrigerator (or freezer) and turn it into something warm and comforting.

Preheat your oven to 350°F (175°C).

Combine the berries, ¼ cup (60 mL) brown sugar and 2 Tbsp (30 mL) flour. Pour into a buttered 8-inch (20 cm) square baking dish.

In a mixing bowl, combine all the remaining ingredients except the butter. Slice the butter into 4 pieces and cut into the dry ingredients with a pastry cutter or a fork. Spread this mixture over the fruit. It will be a little crumbly and not perfectly even but that's just fine. Bake in the oven for 40–45 minutes. Serve while still warm. Perfect topped with good-quality vanilla ice cream.

SERVES 6

PEANUT BUTTER SQUARES

JARED WALLACE, COCHRANE FIRE DEPARTMENT, ALBERTA

FIREFIGHTERS HAVE A great appreciation for the simple things, and fire-fighter Jared Wallace proves this point with his five-ingredient firehouse classic dessert. If you have peanut butter and chocolate you really don't need much else!

In a double boiler melt peanut butter, butter and the chocolate and butterscotch chips. Let cool slightly. Stir in marshmallows and make sure they cover all sides. Spread into a 9 × 13–inch (23 × 33 cm) pan and place in the fridge to cool and set. Cut into squares and serve.

MAKES 9 SQUARES

1 cup (250 mL) peanut butter

½ cup (125 mL) butter

1 cup (250 mL) chocolate chips

1 cup (250 mL) butterscotch or Skor chips

1¼ cups (310 mL) coloured miniature marshmallows

5TH ALARM

SIDES, SAUCES AND THE LITTLE EXTRAS

ALE BAKED
BEANS AND BRISKET

½ lb (225 g) bacon

1 onion, diced

4 garlic cloves, minced

1 tsp (5 mL) ground cumin

1 tsp (5 mL) smoked paprika

1 Tbsp (15 mL) brown sugar

¼ cup (60 mL) ketchup

¼ cup (60 mL) chili sauce

1 Tbsp (15 mL) Dijon mustard

1 Tbsp (15 mL) molasses

¼ cup (60 mL) cider vinegar

4 cups (1 L) ale (I like to use Molson Export)

2 dashes liquid smoke

2 dashes hot sauce

2 drops of Worcestershire

2 cups (500 mL) dried navy beans, rinsed

1 lb (450 g) smoked brisket (deli Montreal smoked meat), cubed

Smoked sea salt, to taste

Freshly ground pepper, to taste

MY GRANDMAMA WAS the best cook I have known and where I continue to draw much of my inspiration from; her recipes are family treasures (that my aunt and I translated to English). She would gracefully feed my large French-Canadian family with ease and a glowing smile on her face, and I'm sure she kept my Grandpapa's firehouse well fed as well. She took great joy in the way food brought people together and the happiness it created. She made amazing baked beans from scratch and served them often for breakfast, lunch and dinner, as well as always having a little pot left over in the refrigerator for any late-night snackers. This comfort food serves well in the firehouse as a stick-to-the-bones side any time of the day and I hope it does her proud!

Preheat the oven to 250°F (120°C).

In a large Dutch oven, sauté the bacon over medium heat until fairly crispy. Reserve the bacon and drain off all but about 2 Tbsp (30 mL) of the bacon fat. Add the diced onion and sauté until soft. Add the garlic, cumin, paprika and brown sugar and sauté for another couple of minutes. Meanwhile, mix together the ketchup, chili sauce, mustard, molasses and vinegar and add it to the Dutch oven. Rinse the mixing cup with some of the ale and add this along with the ale, liquid smoke, hot sauce and Worcestershire to the pot. Once cooled, chop the bacon into bits. Add the beans and bacon bits to the Dutch oven, mixing well; heat to a simmer. Cover the pot and transfer to the oven.

Cook the beans in the oven for about 3½ hours, stirring occasionally, until soft but not falling apart. Add a little more beer if they get too dry during the cooking process. Raise the heat to 400°F (200°C), remove the top, add brisket and cook for another half hour until the sauce becomes thick and caramelized. Season your beans with salt and pepper to taste.

SERVES 4–6

BEER BATTERED
ONION RINGS

MUCH TO DO with the firehouse and our way of life is built around tradition and lore. Change does not happen quickly in the firehouse as our traditions have been passed down for generations. This holds true in our kitchens as well. When I look around my kitchen and see pots and pans from generations past I always think, "Man, if those pots and pans could talk!" The stories that have come out of these pots are ones we still share today.

I have one particular pot in my firehouse that is legendary and definitely has a life of its own. If this pot appeared in anyone's family kitchen it would be ordered to the garbage, but it has a safe home in my firehouse. It's a little shabby, with a crust formed entirely on its outer edges from generations of cooking. You might wonder why not just clean the crust off? Well we have tried that, by sandblasting actually, and it always comes back. This pot is most beloved in our firehouse for the countless batches of delicious stovetop popcorn it has made over the years. Due to its heavy bottom, it also excels at deep frying and I see its legacy growing for generations to come. Our pot is still number one for popcorn but it has now assisted in perfecting batches of Grandpapa's French Fries (see page 168) and these Beer Battered Onion Rings.

You will never be able to make enough of these addictive crunchy onion rings! They are the perfect accompaniment to just about any burger or sammy, and they are well worth the effort.

2 large sweet onions, cut into ½-inch (1 cm) thick slices

4 cups (1 L) canola or peanut oil

2 cups (500 mL) buttermilk

2 cups (500 mL) all-purpose flour, divided

1 tsp (5 mL) garlic powder

1 tsp (5 mL) smoked paprika

Pinch of cayenne

1 tsp (5 mL) kosher salt

Freshly ground pepper, to taste

12 oz (355 mL) bottle of beer, your choice (I prefer an IPA for the hoppy taste)

3 Tbsp (45 mL) finely grated Gruyère cheese

Separate the onions into rings and soak in buttermilk for 1 hour.

In a large Dutch oven or deep fryer heat the oil to 350°F (175°C). This is an important step so use a thermometer.

Whisk together 1 cup (250 mL) flour and all of the seasonings. In a separate bowl whisk together the beer and the other 1 cup (250 mL) flour.

Remove onion rings from the buttermilk and allow any excess to drip off. Dredge in flour, shake off the excess then dip in beer batter. Drop the onion rings in batches in the hot oil, being sure not to crowd rings as they will stick together. When nice and golden remove the rings and allow to drain on paper towels. Sprinkle immediately with Gruyère and salt and pepper.

SERVES 4

GRANDPAPA'S FRENCH FRIES

4-5 medium russet potatoes

4 cups (1 L) lard, duck fat, vegetable oil, peanut oil or any combination of each

1 Tbsp (15 mL) Old Bay seasoning

W E DO LOVE homemade French fries in the firehouse (well, who doesn't) and as it turns out, French fries were a specialty of my Grandpapa, a Quebec City firefighter. His version included potatoes cut precisely by hand and fried in a big pot of lard. Now this might not be for everyone, but it is hard to deny the flavour.

Using a sharp knife slice the potatoes into thin fries, about 3 inches (8 cm) long by ½ inch (1 cm) thick. Transfer the cut potatoes to a large bowl filled with cold water. Swish the potatoes in the water with your hands then drain the water from the potatoes. Refill the bowl with cold water and rinse again. Potatoes can also sit in the water bath overnight. Use paper towels or lint-free kitchen towels to pat dry the potatoes.

Add the lard or oil to a large Dutch oven or heavy-bottomed pot over low heat to render if necessary. Put the potatoes into cold rendered fat or oil. Place the oven on the stove and turn the heat to medium-high. Cook the potatoes for 25–30 minutes until crisp and golden brown on the outside and tender inside, stirring occasionally. The oil will bubble briskly once it comes to heat. Line a baking sheet with paper towels and set aside. Use a spider or slotted spoon to scoop out the fries and transfer them to the baking sheet. Immediately sprinkle the fries with Old Bay.

 SERVES 4–6

BEET RISOTTO

It is tough to "beet" the appearance of this dish, as the shredded beets produce a vibrant colour and taste. Wear an apron while making this one!

Peel the beets and coarsely shred 2 of them. Thinly slice the third beet and set it aside for garnish.

In a saucepan bring the stock to a simmer. Add the herbs and garlic, cover and keep warm. In a large cast iron braising pan melt the butter in the oil. Add the onion and cook over medium heat, stirring until softened, about 5 minutes. Add the shredded beets and cook, stirring, until the pan is dry. Deglaze the pan with the wine and simmer until all is absorbed. Spoon half of the beets into a small bowl and set aside.

Add the rice to the pan and cook, stirring for 2 minutes until fragrant. Add 1 cup (250 mL) of the warm stock to the rice and cook over moderate heat, stirring, until the stock is nearly absorbed. Continue adding the stock 1 cup (250 mL) at a time, stirring constantly until the rice is al dente and a thick sauce forms, about 20 minutes. Stir in the cooked beets and the cheese. Cook and stir until heated through, adding a few tablespoons of stock if the risotto is too thick. Season the risotto to taste with salt and pepper then spoon the risotto into bowls. Garnish with sliced beets, shavings of pecorino and fresh parsley.

SERVES 4

3 large beets (¾ lb/375 g each)

8 cups (2 L) vegetable stock

¼ cup (60 mL) of assorted fresh herbs, such as thyme, basil or oregano

2 cloves garlic, crushed

¼ cup (60 mL) unsalted butter

¼ cup (60 mL) extra virgin olive oil

1 large sweet onion, finely chopped

½ cup (125 mL) dry white wine

3 cups (750 mL) arborio rice

1 cup (250 mL) young pecorino cheese, freshly grated + more shaved, for garnish

Kosher salt, to taste

Freshly ground pepper, to taste

¼ cup (60 mL) freshly chopped flat-leaf parsley, for garnish

COCONUT SAFFRON RICE PILAF

Pinch of saffron

1 Tbsp (15 mL) hot water

2 Tbsp (30 mL) coconut oil

½ cup (125 mL) chopped onion

¼ cup (60 mL) chopped
red bell pepper

2 Tbsp (30 mL) minced shallots

1 tsp (5 mL) minced garlic

1¼ cups (310 mL)
basmati rice

1½ cups (375 mL) vegetable
stock

½ cup (125 mL) coconut milk

½ cup (125 mL) coconut cream

1 tsp (5 mL) turmeric

1 tsp (5 mL) garam masala

Kosher salt, to taste

Freshly ground pepper, to taste

¼ cup (60 mL) chopped
fresh cilantro

It is easy to give rice an exotic feel with a few ingredient additions from the pantry. Serve this as an accompaniment to any grilled meat or fish or serve as a vegetarian main course.

In a small bowl soak the saffron threads in hot (not boiling) water for at least 5 minutes to release their flavour. Heat the coconut oil in a large saucepan over medium-high heat. Add the onion, bell pepper, shallots and garlic and cook stirring for about 2 minutes. Add the rice, stir to coat with the oil and cook for 1 minute. Add the vegetable stock, coconut milk, coconut cream, saffron and water, turmeric, garam masala, salt and pepper. Bring the mixture to a light boil. Reduce the heat to low, cover and simmer until the rice is tender and all the liquid is absorbed, about 20 minutes.

Remove from the heat and let sit 10 minutes. Fluff with a fork and stir in the cilantro.

SERVES 6 AS A SIDE, 4 AS A MAIN

CREAMED SPINACH
WITH ARTICHOKE

SOMETIMES IT TAKES a little disguising to get firefighters to eat their vegetables, but you can make anyone love spinach with this recipe! It is the perfect accompaniment to a grilled steak, or you can double it up to make a party dip.

Cook the spinach in a pot of boiling water for just 1 minute, add to cold water bath to stop the cooking then squeeze out the excess water from the leaves. Chop the spinach (or throw in a food processor to blend) and set aside.

Melt the butter in a large saucepan over medium heat. Add the garlic and onion and cook until just soft, about 5 minutes. Add the artichokes and toss to coat them well with the onion and garlic. Add in the flour, stirring it constantly to form a paste, and cook for a couple of minutes. Slowly whisk in the milk and cook until slightly thickened, about 3–5 minutes. Stir in the Parmesan and add in the spinach. Season with nutmeg, salt and pepper and stir for a couple of minutes to warm everything through. Serve right away.

SERVES 6 AS A SIDE

3½ cups (875 mL) baby spinach

¼ cup (60 mL) unsalted butter

2 garlic cloves, grated

1 onion, diced

Two 14-oz (410 mL) cans artichoke hearts, roughly chopped

3 Tbsp (45 mL) all-purpose flour

2 cups (500 mL) milk

½ cup (125 mL) grated Parmesan cheese

½ tsp (2 mL) nutmeg

Kosher salt, to taste

Freshly ground pepper, to taste

GERMAN POTATO-SALAD
WEDGES SUPREME

2 lb (900 g) russet potatoes, cut into quarter-long wedges

2 Tbsp (30 mL) olive oil

1 tsp (5 mL) kosher salt + more to taste

Freshly ground pepper, to taste

½ lb (225 g) thick-cut bacon

¾ cup (190 mL) finely chopped sweet onion

⅓ cup (80 mL) white wine vinegar

¼ cup (60 mL) sugar

2 Tbsp (30 mL) Dijon mustard

½ cup (125 mL) coarsely grated spiced gouda

2 Tbsp (30 mL) minced chives, for garnish

1 bunch green onions, chopped, for garnish

2 hard boiled eggs, chopped, for garnish

½ cup (125 mL) chopped dill pickles, for garnish

IF OKTOBERFEST DECONSTRUCTED the classic potato salad served at Feast Halls across Kitchener and Waterloo and reinvented a fries supreme, then this would be the recipe! Makes a great side show to the Oktoberfest Burger (see page 84) or it can be served as a fun main course at a party.

Preheat oven to 400°F (200°C). Place the potatoes on a baking tray lined with parchment paper and toss with the olive oil, salt and pepper. Cook until potatoes are crisp on the outside and tender in the middle, approximately 30 minutes.

Cook the bacon in a large skillet over medium-high heat. Once crisp, place on a paper towel–lined plate and crumble into small pieces. Pour off the rendered fat, reserving ¼ cup (60 mL) in the pan. Turn the heat to medium and add the onion. Cook until soft and just beginning to brown, about 4–5 minutes.

Whisk in the vinegar, sugar, mustard and a pinch of salt and stir until thick and bubbly. Keep warm.

When the potato wedges are done cooking remove them from the oven and drizzle all over with the warm dressing. Garnish your wedges with the bacon, gouda, chives, green onions, eggs and pickles.

SERVES 6 AS A SIDE DISH

POMMES ALIGOT

WE LOVE COMFORT food in the firehouse and if you are a fan of mashed potatoes then you have to give this recipe a try—an indulgent French comfort food with cheesy ribbon-like mashed potatoes. Get your wooden spoon out for this one!

Put potatoes in a pot of cold salted water, turn heat to high and bring to a boil. Lower heat to a simmer and cook until potatoes can be pierced easily with a knife, about 20 minutes. Drain.

Put potatoes and garlic in a food processor and pulse until smooth.

Scoop potatoes back into pot. Over low heat, stir in the butter and cream with a wooden spoon. Season the potatoes generously with salt and pepper. Stir in the cheeses 1 cup (250 mL) at a time until potatoes achieve a ribbon-like consistency when you scoop them up with your wooden spoon. Top with fresh parsley and serve immediately.

SERVES 6 AS A SIDE

8 Yukon Gold potatoes, peeled

Kosher salt, to taste

3 cloves of garlic, peeled

¾ cup (190 mL) unsalted butter, at room temperature

1½ cups (375 mL) heavy cream, warmed

Freshly ground pepper, to taste

1½ cups (375 mL) grated fresh mozzarella

1½ cups (375 mL) grated Gruyère

½ cup (125 mL) grated raclette cheese

¼ cup (60 mL) fresh flat-leaf parsley, for garnish

ROASTED BRUSSELS SPROUTS WITH PANCETTA, WALNUTS AND PARMESAN

WHEN SHIFTS AT the firehouse fall over the holidays we still try to celebrate as if we were at home. A potluck style is our way of getting everyone from the crew involved, and this side of Brussels sprouts is a wonderful accompaniment to holiday dinners (or as a warm salad).

Preheat the oven to 450°F (230°C).

Toss the Brussels sprouts with 2 Tbsp (30 mL) olive oil and sprinkle with salt and pepper on a rimmed baking tray. Spread the Brussels sprouts out on the baking tray and roast, stirring once or twice during the cooking process, until tender and charred in spots, about 30 minutes.

Meanwhile add the pancetta to a medium sauté pan and render over medium heat for about 4 minutes. Add the remaining olive oil, walnuts, garlic, shallots and a pinch of salt. Cook until the bacon is crispy, being careful not to burn the walnuts. Stir in the vinegar, honey, mustard and Parmesan. Whisk everything together into the bacon fat until emulsified and taste for seasoning. Toss the roasted Brussels sprouts with the bacon-walnut mixture until well coated.

SERVES 6 AS A SIDE

1½ lb (700 g) Brussels sprouts, halved

3 Tbsp (45 mL) extra virgin olive oil, divided

Kosher salt, to taste

Freshly ground black pepper, to taste

½ lb (225 g) pancetta, cut into 1-inch (2.5 cm) pieces

½ cup (125 mL) walnuts, coarsely chopped

2 garlic cloves, sliced

2 shallots, sliced

2 Tbsp (30 mL) red wine vinegar

1 Tbsp (15 mL) honey

1 Tbsp (15 mL) grainy mustard

2 Tbsp (30 mL) finely grated Parmesan cheese

AVOCADO LIME CREMA

4 avocados, peeled, pitted and chopped

2 cups (500 mL) crema or thick sour cream

Juice and zest of 1 lime

1 jalapeño pepper, seeded, chopped

A few drops of green Tabasco sauce + more to taste

¼ cup (60 mL) fresh cilantro, chopped

Kosher salt, to taste

Freshly ground pepper, to taste

Crema is a velvety and rich 35% sour cream. With the addition of avocado and lime this sauce is the perfect tangy and cool topper to just about anything Mexican, or you can use it anywhere you would use regular sour cream.

Using a food processor pulse all of the ingredients together until just smooth, then season with salt and pepper. Crema will keep in the refrigerator for up to a week.

MAKES 3 CUPS (750 ML)

CHIMICHURRI SAUCE

1 cup (250 mL) lightly packed fresh flat-leaf parsley

½ cup (125 mL) lightly packed fresh cilantro

3-5 garlic cloves, minced

1 tsp (5 mL) kosher salt

1 tsp (5 mL) freshly ground pepper

1 tsp (5 mL) chili pepper flakes

2 Tbsp (30 mL) fresh oregano

2 Tbsp (30 mL) minced green onion

¾ cup (190 mL) grapeseed oil

3 Tbsp (45 mL) sherry wine vinegar

3 Tbsp (45 mL) lemon juice

My wife and I began jarring this super-versatile and flavourful sauce because we loved it so much on just about everything. It made its way into my firehouse and before I knew it recipes were being created just to find things to put it on. It is zingy, highly flavourful and adds brightness to just about any dish.

Place all ingredients in a food processor and pulse until well chopped, but not puréed. Taste and adjust seasoning if necessary. Place in a glass screw-top mason jar and use on everything!

MAKES ABOUT 2 CUPS (500 ML)

CREOLE REMOULADE SAUCE

¾ cup (190 mL) mayonnaise

¼ cup (60 mL) grapeseed oil

½ cup (125 mL) chopped green onions

1 medium onion, chopped

¼ cup (60 mL) fresh lemon juice

1 stalk of celery, chopped

2 Tbsp (30 mL) grainy Dijon mustard

1 Tbsp (15 mL) honey mustard

3 Tbsp (45 mL) ketchup

2 Tbsp (30 mL) chili sauce

3 Tbsp (45 mL) chopped flat-leaf parsley leaves

2 garlic cloves

2 Tbsp (30 mL) horseradish

2 Tbsp (30 mL) capers

1 tsp (5 mL) salt

¼ tsp (1 mL) cayenne

¼ tsp (1 mL) paprika

¼ tsp (1 mL) freshly ground black pepper

USE THIS CLASSIC sauce from French cuisine to give any seafood a kick, particularly if it's fried. You can also use this as a spread to take your sandwiches to the next level.

In a blender or food processor, combine all ingredients and process until fairly smooth, about 30 seconds or so. Store in a sealable jar in the refrigerator for up to 2 weeks.

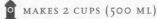 MAKES 2 CUPS (500 ML)

PICO DE GALLO

4 large Roma tomatoes, chopped

1 jalapeño, minced

1 garlic clove, minced

1 red onion, minced

Juice of 1 lime

¼ cup (60 mL) fresh cilantro, chopped

1 Tbsp (15 mL) extra virgin olive oil

Kosher salt, to taste

Freshly ground pepper, to taste

MAKE A BATCH of this easy and super-fresh salsa and you will notice the difference that only homemade can make!

In a bowl mix all the ingredients. Keep in a covered container in the refrigerator for up to a week.

 MAKES I CUP (250 ML)

QUICK PEANUT SAUCE

An authentic Thai-inspired dipping sauce that's great for satays, spring rolls or even as a dressing for salad.

Place all ingredients in a blender or food processor. Blend or process until sauce is smooth.

Do a taste test, adding more fish sauce (or soy sauce) if not salty enough, or more cayenne if not spicy enough. If too salty, add a squeeze of fresh lime juice. If you'd prefer it sweeter, add a little more sugar.

MAKES 2 CUPS (500 ML)

1 cup (250 mL) dry roasted unsalted peanuts

⅓ cup (80 mL) water

2 garlic cloves, minced

½ tsp (2 mL) dark soy sauce

2 tsp (10 mL) sesame oil

1–2 Tbsp (15–30 mL) brown sugar

2 Tbsp (30 mL) fish sauce

½ tsp (2 mL) fresh lime juice

½ tsp (2 mL) cayenne

⅓ cup (80 mL) coconut milk

BBQ BOURBON GLAZE

Bourbon gives this sweet and spicy BBQ glaze a nice smoky touch. It is made to finish off the Bacon-Wrapped Chicken Wings (see page 2) but it's perfect for anything that touches the grill.

Combine all ingredients in a small saucepan and simmer for 10 minutes over low-medium heat.

MAKES ABOUT 2 CUPS (500 ML)

3 Tbsp (45 mL) butter

¼ cup (60 mL) brown sugar

4 cloves of garlic, finely chopped

½ tsp (2 mL) prepared horseradish

¼ tsp (1 mL) ground ginger

¼ cup (60 mL) soy sauce

½ cup (125 mL) bourbon

¾ cup (190 mL) ketchup

A few dashes of hot sauce

ROMESCO SAUCE

¼ cup (60 mL) ground almonds

12 oz (355 mL) jar roasted red peppers, drained

3 Tbsp (45 mL) olive oil

2 Tbsp (30 mL) sherry vinegar

¼ tsp (1 mL) cayenne

1 slice white bread, crusts removed, toasted and torn into pieces

1 large clove garlic, grated

Kosher salt, to taste

Freshly cracked black pepper, to taste

Tʜɪs ʀᴏᴀsᴛᴇᴅ ʀᴇᴅ pepper sauce offers amazing colour and zip to just about any dish. You can dip it, spread it or use it in place of pasta sauce.

In a food processor add the almonds, red peppers, olive oil, vinegar, cayenne, bread and garlic. Process until the mixture is smooth and season with salt and pepper.

MAKES 1 CUP (250 ML)

SIMPLE TOMATO SAUCE

1 Tbsp (15 mL) extra virgin olive oil

1 large sweet onion, chopped

Kosher salt, to taste

¼ cup (60 mL) red wine

28 oz (796 mL) can San Marzano tomatoes

1 Tbsp (15 mL) dried oregano

1 Tbsp (15 mL) dried basil

1 Tbsp (15 mL) dried thyme

Hot sauce, to taste

1 Tbsp (15 mL) balsamic vinegar

Freshly ground pepper, to taste

Tʜɪs ʀᴇᴄɪᴘᴇ ɪs made for the firehouse! Think of it as a blank slate—it can be used for anything from pasta to sandwiches, as a base for other sauces or you can even poach eggs in it. Keeping a jar of this simple, flavourful tomato sauce in the fridge makes busy night shift meals a delicious breeze.

Coat the bottom of a pot with olive oil and place over medium heat. Add the onion with a sprinkle of salt and cook until the onion is soft and translucent, about 5 minutes. Add the red wine and cook until all the liquid is absorbed. Add tomatoes, oregano, basil and thyme and bring to a simmer. Stir in the hot sauce and balsamic vinegar. Maintain a low simmer for at least 15 minutes until the sauce thickens and the flavours really come together. With a hand blender purée sauce until smooth. Taste sauce and season with salt and pepper if necessary.

MAKES ABOUT 4 CUPS (1 L)

SRIRACHA AIOLI

I LOVE WHEN my firehouse crew takes the recipes I create home with them. When I write recipes, my goal is to get people back in the kitchen cooking. I remember when I made my first batch of Sriracha Aioli one of my brothers at the firehouse paid very close attention to the method; he went home, made a batch of his own for his family, came back to the firehouse next shift and told me this sauce changed his life! His family loved it and couldn't stop putting it on absolutely everything. To me, that is what cooking is all about!

There have been countless firehouse recipes created just to try and find something to put this aioli on. It all started with the Jalapeño Kettle Chip Fish Tacos (see page 79), but now it's used as a dip for pretty much anything left in the refrigerator, or as a spread to fire-up any sandwich (including peanut butter!). It's perfect on the now famous 3-Meat 3-Heat Burger (see page 68) and an extra-large batch is always made just to help us get through a shift. Let your creativity and taste buds guide you to different uses for this simple and highly flavoured sauce.

In a bowl, mix all the ingredients. Aioli will keep in the refrigerator for up to a week.

MAKES ABOUT I CUP (250 ML), SO YOU BETTER DOUBLE IT!

1 cup (250 mL) mayonnaise

3 Tbsp (45 mL) sriracha sauce

1 Tbsp (15 mL) grated garlic

Kosher salt, to taste

Freshly ground pepper, to taste

LEMON CAPER AIOLI

WITH THE ADDITION of fresh citrus zest and briny capers, this aioli is a great accompaniment to anything seafood as a dip or spread.

Combine all ingredients in a bowl and season to taste with salt and pepper. Aioli will keep up to a week in the refrigerator.

MAKES ABOUT I CUP (250 ML)

1 cup (250 mL) mayonnaise

1 lemon, juiced and zested

2 Tbsp (30 mL) capers, finely chopped

1 Tbsp (15 mL) grated garlic

Kosher salt, to taste

Freshly ground pepper, to taste

GREEK TZATZIKI DIP

JARED WALLACE, COCHRANE FIRE DEPARTMENT,
ALBERTA

2 cucumbers, peeled,
seeded and grated

½ tsp (2 mL) kosher salt +
more to taste

2 cups (500 mL) plain
Greek yogurt

2 Tbsp (30 mL) fresh squeezed
lemon juice

2 garlic cloves, minced

2 Tbsp (30 mL) extra virgin
olive oil

Freshly ground pepper,
to taste

GREAT RECIPES ARE meant to be shared, and firefighter Jared Wallace's recipes have become a hit in his firehouse. Homemade is always better and Jared makes his tzatziki shine by using natural yogurt with active bacteria for a better texture. Enjoy Jared's homemade tzatziki as a dip for crudités, fresh veggies, pitas or as a spread on sandwiches.

Place grated cucumber in a colander and sprinkle with salt. Let the moisture drain from the cucumbers for 10–15 minutes. Squeeze any excess moisture from cucumber by wrapping in a paper towel.

In a bowl combine cucumber, yogurt, lemon juice and garlic. Mix in olive oil and salt and pepper to taste. Refrigerate for 2 hours. Serve with wedges of pita bread or mixed fresh vegetables.

MAKES ABOUT 2 CUPS (500 ML)

SUPER STEEL CUT OATS WITH BLUEBERRIES AND DARK CHOCOLATE

IF YOU NEED energy for the day, as we do in the firehouse, then this warm and hearty breakfast is a great start and will help carry you through. Make a double batch, as it keeps well for up to a week in the refrigerator.

Melt the butter in a medium saucepan over medium heat. Add the oats and stir continuously until they smell nice and nutty, about 3 minutes. Add water, almond milk, syrup and salt. Turn up the heat and bring to a simmer. Cover and cook for 20 minutes, stirring occasionally to keep the oats from sticking to the bottom of the pan. Remove the lid and stir in the walnuts, blueberries and dark chocolate. Cover again and cook for about 10 more minutes, stirring on occasion, until the oats are soft and creamy.

SERVES 4–6

1 Tbsp (15 mL) unsalted butter

1 cup (250 mL) steel-cut oats

3 cups (750 mL) water

1 cup (250 mL) almond milk

2 Tbsp (30 mL) agave syrup or maple syrup

½ tsp (2 mL) kosher salt

½ cup (125 mL) crushed walnuts

2 cups (500 mL) blueberries

¼ cup (60 mL) dark chocolate shavings (preferably 70% or more cocoa)

BETH'S BEST WHITE ROLLS

BETH EDWARDS, EXECUTIVE DIRECTOR, FIREFIGHTERS
ASSOCIATION OF NOVA SCOTIA

1 cup (250 mL) warm water

½ cup (125 mL) + 2 tsp
(10 mL) sugar

2½ Tbsp (37 mL) regular yeast

12 cups (3 L) flour

2 tsp (10 mL) kosher salt

2 eggs

¼ cup (60 mL) oil + more
for greasing

7-8 cups (1.75-2 L) water +
more for kneading

Butter, for greasing and
smearing

YOU CANNOT BEAT the aroma of fresh baked bread wafting through the firehouse or your home. Your crew or guests will taste the love and effort put into making these homemade rolls—thanks to Beth!

Make sure the water is not too hot, just warm. In a bowl mix 2 tsp (10 mL) sugar with the warm water. Stir in the regular yeast, mix well and cover the bowl with a dish towel; let sit 10–15 minutes until a foam forms.

In a separate bowl mix together the flour with the remaining sugar and salt.

In a third bowl mix together the eggs, oil and water. Mix in with dry mixture. You might need to keep adding flour until you get a decent dough to handle and roll, so experiment. Don't let the dough be soupy, just keep throwing the flour at it until it is just a little tacky but doesn't stick.

Knead dough for 10–15 minutes, and oil up a large bowl. Put the dough in the greased bowl and poke down with fingers, turn over and poke down again. Cover with plastic wrap and tuck over dough a little—make it snug. Wrap in a kitchen garbage bag and throw a couple of tea towels over it. Let the dough rise undisturbed for about 1 hour.

For the second rise, just punch the dough down with the tea towels still on it. If you're at home, time to grab the wine! Let the dough rise again for 1 hour, then it's ready to put into pans.

Roll into balls and put into greased muffin pans or a greased bread pan.

Cover up in the pan with tea towels or plastic wrap. After about 1 hour shove into the oven and bake at 475°F (240°C) for 15–17 minutes. Remove from the oven, get the butter ready and smear the top of the rolls with butter. I find 17 minutes is best but obviously if the rolls are made bigger you can bake to about 19 minutes.

MAKES 24 ROLLS

GARBAGE BAG WHOLE-WHEAT BREAD

BETH EDWARDS, EXECUTIVE DIRECTOR, FIREFIGHTERS
ASSOCIATION OF NOVA SCOTIA

BETH HAS DEFINITELY perfected bread making with this recipe, and she makes the most of the time-consuming process by enjoying the occasional glass of wine! She shares this Nova Scotian "garbage bag" method for a delicious loaf.

5 cups (1.25 L) whole-wheat flour

5 cups (1.25 L) white flour

4-5 Tbsp (60-75 mL) salt

Little over ½ cup (125 mL) of lard, cut up

1 cup (250 mL) warm water

2 tsp (10 mL) sugar

2½ Tbsp (37 mL) active dry yeast

4 cups (1 L) lukewarm water (approx.)

2 Tbsp (30 mL) butter

Mix together the flours, salt and lard; mix with your hands to incorporate and set aside.

Make sure the water is not too hot, just warm. In a bowl mix sugar with the warm water. Stir in the yeast, mix well and cover the bowl with a dish towel; let sit 10–15 minutes until a foam forms.

Stir yeast mixture into flour. Add enough lukewarm water to form a dough. Knead a little then let the dough sit on the counter for 10–15 minutes to rest. The beauty of this recipe is you don't have to knead for very long, just about 5 minutes. If it's the afternoon, pour a glass of red wine (optional).

Put the dough in a greased bowl, dab with lard and poke down with fingers. Now, here comes the fun part—wrap a piece of plastic over the dough then take a garbage bag and wrap the bowl up and tie the ends of the garbage bag off. Cover with a couple of tea towels and let rise for about 1 hour.

After the first rising knead dough for about 5 minutes then poke again, let rise again with the dough wrapped up in a garbage bag again and let rise for another hour.

Cover your fingers in lard and use your hands to form dough into 2 balls; place both balls on a greased bread pan. Cover and rise again for 45–60 minutes. This is the third and last rising (pour more wine if needed). Preheat oven to 350°F (175°C) and place the pan into oven for 35–40 minutes.

Take bread out, rub 1 Tbsp (15 mL) of butter on top each loaf, and remove from pans. Let cool then enjoy.

Hint: this bread freezes really well too!

MAKES 2 LOAVES OF BREAD

CRETON

THIS CLASSIC QUEBEC breakfast spread resembles a pâté and is one of my fondest memories of my Grandmama, Grandpapa and Quebec family. I can still smell my Grandmama's kitchen as if she were making it today, with warm spices and ground pork simmering together for hours. Breakfast was never complete without a jar of creton at the table! It is now a treat in my firehouse and I couldn't be prouder to carry on my Grandmama's love and passion for food. Enjoy it as a spread on toast topped with the traditional yellow mustard.

In a saucepan over medium heat melt the butter and sweat the onion and garlic until just soft, about 5 minutes. Soak the breadcrumbs in the milk while the vegetables are softening. Add the pork, soaked breadcrumbs, spices, salt and pepper. Cover and simmer all ingredients for about 1 hour, stirring occasionally, then uncover and simmer until all the liquid has evaporated. Put into individual ramekins or a decorative dish and refrigerate to set.

To serve, spread generously on toast and top with yellow mustard. Enjoy!

MAKES ABOUT 2½ CUPS (625 ML)

¼ cup (60 mL) butter

1 onion, grated

1 clove garlic, grated

1 cup (250 mL) fresh breadcrumbs

1 cup (250 mL) milk

1 lb (450 g) lean ground pork

½ tsp (2 mL) ground cinnamon

½ tsp (2 mL) ground ginger

½ tsp (2 mL) ground nutmeg

½ tsp (2 mL) ground cloves

Kosher salt, to taste

Freshly ground pepper, to taste

1 loaf of your favourite bread, toasted, for serving

Yellow mustard, for serving

CREDITS

On Feb 4, 2007, the Winnipeg Fire Department tragically lost two of its members, Captains Tom Nicholls and Harold Lessard, to a house fire. Jeff Derraugh proudly had the privilege of dedicating his first cookbook, *Fire Hall Cooking with Jeff the Chef* to Harold and Tom.

Five Star Whisky Brisket (page 112) was originally published in *Fire Hall Cooking with Jeff the Chef*, TouchWood Editions (2007), and is republished with permission.

Jeff's second cookbook, *Where There's Food There's Firefighters* was dedicated to all the fallen firefighters who made the ultimate sacrifice. This tribute recognizes brothers and sisters taken while on duty, as well as those who succumbed to the silent firefighter killers of heart disease and occupational cancers. During this time the United Firefighters of Winnipeg were laying the groundwork for a Manitoba Fallen Firefighters Memorial and Jeff directed all profits from his cookbook towards the memorial fund.

Taco Chicken Soup (page 44) and Fallin'-Off-the-Bone-Already Ribs (page 94) were originally published in *Where There's Food, There's Firefighters*, Touch-Wood Editions (2009), and are republished with permission.

Additional photography for Hungarian Goulash with Dumplings (page 98) and Stout Chocolate Cake (page 157) by Sarah Graham, www.saragraham-photography.com

INDEX